# If These
# WALLS
## Could TALK:
## BALTIMORE ORIOLES

T0164277

# *If These* **WALLS** *Could* **TALK:**

## BALTIMORE ORIOLES

### Stories from the Baltimore Orioles Dugout, Locker Room, and Press Box

Rick Dempsey with Dave Ginsburg

**TRIUMPH**
**B O O K S**

Library of Congress Cataloging-in-Publication Data

Names: Dempsey, Rick. | Ginsburg, Dave.

Title: If these walls could talk, Baltimore Orioles : stories from the Baltimore Orioles sideline, locker room, and press box / by Rick Dempsey with Dave Ginsburg.

Description: Chicago, Illinois : Triumph Books, 2017.

Identifiers: LCCN 2016050690 | ISBN 9781629373447 (paperback)

Subjects: LCSH: Baltimore Orioles (Baseball team)—History. | Baltimore Orioles (Baseball team)—Anecdotes. | BISAC: SPORTS & RECREATION / Baseball / General. | TRAVEL / United States / South / South Atlantic (DC, DE, FL, GA, MD, NC, SC, VA, WV).

Classification: LCC GV875.B2 .D46 2017 | DDC 796.357/64097526—dc23

LC record available at https://lccn.loc.gov/2016050690

This book is available in quantity at special discounts for your group or organization. For further information, contact:

**Triumph Books LLC**
814 North Franklin Street
Chicago, Illinois 60610
(312) 337-0747
www.triumphbooks.com


Printed in U.S.A.

ISBN: 978-1-62937-344-7

Design by Amy Carter

*To Harmon Killebrew and Brooks Robinson, two of the finest people I've ever met, and all my wonderful teammates over the years.*

*And to Cal Ripken Jr., Eddie Murray, and Orel Hershiser, outstanding players who helped me win a couple of World Series rings.*

*And to my wife, Joani, who has provided guidance and patience throughout my career in baseball, both as a player and on television.*

# CONTENTS

# FOREWORD

The Orioles were the model organization when I was a kid. I remember my dad being part of it and taking pride in knowing they were good from top to bottom. They developed a lot of players in the minor league system, and I had a chance to witness that. My dad, Cal Sr., was a manager there for 14 years. To see the instruction, the pride, and players going from the minor leagues up to the major leagues to become superstars, it was really fun to be a part of it. There was a special pride the Orioles had in their baseball know-how, the organization, and the system, and it really showcased itself at the top. That organization was about winning in the big leagues. Along the way you won in the minor leagues, but it was more about developing good baseball players who knew how to play the game.

As a kid I remember going to spring training and listening to my dad address the minor league group. What stuck with me were his opening remarks. He said, "The Baltimore Orioles are the greatest organization in baseball. If you get through our organization, you will play in the big leagues. It might not be with the Orioles, but you will play in the big leagues." That was sort of a philosophy, or ideology, that everybody aspired to.

It was easy for me to see this from the inside. As a kid who grew up in the Baltimore area, I loved Brooks Robinson, loved the quality of the team each and every year. It was exciting. To have the dream to be a pro baseball player, and on top of that, having the dream of playing with the Baltimore Orioles, made it even more special.

I know that the Yankees have their history and all those World Series titles. If you pay attention to baseball history, you understand where their place is and how dominant they were. But as a kid, to me, you could look at the Orioles and say they were as dominant as any team in the game. The Dodgers were considered that way, too, but it was a special feeling, being around Baltimore. It was even better being on the inside, seeing it through Dad's eyes and what his value was to the organization. The Orioles were just a wonderful organization, and it was great to have a team so close by that you could really take pride in.

After being drafted by the Orioles in 1978, I went through the minor league system, and it seemed some of the ideology had changed a little bit. My dad had gone to the big leagues when I was a junior in high school. Going through the minor league system, there was still a good feeling about what The Oriole Way was—how to play the game and learn the game— but some new concepts were being introduced from other people coming into the organization. I didn't think it was working the same way that it used to, but it was still working pretty well when I went through the system. I had a chance to learn, I had a chance to gain experience, and I got through it one step at a time. Being 17 years old, I was pretty wide-eyed going into the minor leagues because you were measuring yourself against people who played in college and were older than you. But having grown up in the Orioles family, I knew a little bit more about what to expect, and that ultimately helped me out quite a bit.

I came through the system pretty quickly. I was in Rochester, about to turn 21 later that summer in 1981, and that was the year they had a strike. There was some talk about bringing me up because Doug DeCinces got hurt early in that season. However, with the strike looming, they elected to keep me down there to continue developing in Triple A. Once the strike was over, they expanded the rosters by two, and I got one of the two spots. Coming into the big leagues, I was excited. I didn't have a chance to play regularly but got my feet wet. I didn't play particularly well, didn't hit particularly well. I was a little nervous, a little scared. And then after that, I went to winter ball to regain my confidence and my swing, and that went perfectly. While I was in winter ball they traded DeCinces to the Angels, and that opened up a spot at third for me.

Coming into the next spring training, I felt like more a part of the team. I swung the bat pretty well in spring training and became the starting third baseman. I went 3-for-5 on Opening Day, including a home run in my first at-bat. Then I went four for my next 63. So that's 7-for-68. Not great. But this is a side of Earl Weaver that most people don't see: he was pretty empathetic to my situation. He was even nurturing in some ways. He would call me into his office all the time and he always said what was on his mind. But most of all, the message was, "You figured out how to do it in the minor leagues, you did it in winter ball. There's nothing more you have to prove down there. You just have to be yourself up here."

It took a little while, but I'll always be thankful to Earl Weaver because he was a manager who had enough confidence in what he knew, and he would stick to what he knew. If I played for a different manager or a new manager, they might have thought that I needed to go back down and regain my confidence and work out my problems in Triple A. But Earl kept me in the lineup and kept pushing me through. Once I found it, I found it really big. That was in 1982, the year we missed going to the playoffs by losing to the

Brewers in Game 162. But it was a really gratifying season for me because I established myself and got my feet on the ground. I was voted Rookie of the Year.

Once you feel like you're established and you can play at this level, it made it a whole lot easier for me to come to the ballpark. Things went well in 1983, especially in the second half. We won the World Series, I caught the final out, and I was voted AL MVP.

During that time frame, the definition of an everyday player was someone like Eddie Murray. He had a streak of his own. Brooks Robinson played in 483 straight games. So the expectation, if you were one of the key players, was to play. My dad said your job is to come to the ballpark ready to play, and if your manager chooses to use you, you play. It's really interesting when I look at my streak and how it was perceived. There were times when people would take a negative position on it. But the streak was created by the likes of Earl Weaver, Joe Altobelli, Frank Robinson, and even my dad, who also managed the team.

The manager sits in that room and makes the lineup every night. And it was a huge compliment to be thought of as someone who could help the team win the game. It wasn't my job to say I needed an off day; it was my job to respond to the manager's wishes.

All of a sudden, the streak got to 1,000 games without much talk, and it was all about responding to the day-to-day challenge of getting ready to play. To my manager I was performing and deserving of being in the lineup. During that time we went through a major rebuilding process, and fingers were pointed at everybody. There were times when I was slumping, and the streak would become an issue. There was a lot of negativity then, but when the streak got to 1,700-1,800 games, all the critics became people who really thought it was a great thing. I never quite understood how or why people's opinions flipped when the streak reached a certain number.

Then, finally, once it got close to 2,000 games and people started to assume I was really going to break Lou Gehrig's record of 2,130 games, it became something that was good for baseball. But to me, it was all the same: just showing up to the park ready to play one game at a time. Knowing how the Orioles operated and the lessons I got from my dad, it was an honor to be an everyday player. To perform every day, it was what I thought was right.

Much of the streak took place while the Orioles were rebuilding. We lost 21 straight games to start the season in 1988. There were changes in the organization. I could have left Baltimore, but I looked at it and evaluated the situation and thought I was young enough to withstand the rebuilding process, which is not fun for the fans or the players. It's much easier to play on a winner. It's difficult to try to bring the same approach, the same level of enthusiasm and passion every day when you're losing. But I always stuck to it.

The nights of September 5 and 6, 1995, were wonderful celebrations. People often ask me what my favorite moment of my career was. I tell them that catching the final out of the 1983 World Series was the greatest baseball moment and the culmination of an amazing season for the team and the city. Games 2,130 and 2,131 were my favorite, and they were very human moments, ones that I am so grateful for.

Ultimately, I figured all good things have to come to an end at some point. I felt like there was another rebuilding process coming up, so I thought maybe it was time to start anew. It was time to end the streak. I was going to do it on the last day of the 1998 season in Boston. It was, almost as if to say, "Look, I could have played in 162 if I wanted" because I took pride in being able to do that.

People close to me suggested that I do it in Baltimore, where people appreciated the streak and what it took to make it happen. They said, "Make it a positive." It was exactly the right advice. So I chose the last game of the home schedule for a game against the Yankees. I waited until 10 minutes before the game started. I told manager Ray Miller, who passed that on to the press box. I didn't want any fanfare beforehand. It unfolded as a celebration of a principle as opposed to the ending of the streak. That was really important to me. During the game I didn't know what to do with myself. For the first time in what seemed like forever, I felt like I was on the outside looking in as opposed to being in the middle of the game. Quite honestly, I didn't like it.

I do remember I had to talk backup third baseman Ryan Minor into taking the field because he thought it was a prank. The Yankees realized what was happening and stood on top of the dugout and applauded, which made it that much more special.

It was hard going through the rebuilding process. I would have liked to have been on more championship teams, I would have liked being in the playoffs more. The Orioles have gone through many different changes in an effort to turn things around, but I'm really happy about the state of the organization now. I always thought Buck Showalter was one of the best base-ball minds in the game. I had a chance to know him, talk to him, and examine plays with him while working in television. He fit in with Baltimore perfectly. He took a lot of responsibility for a lot of things. I know executive vice president of baseball operations Dan Duquette has played a nice role in putting together teams for Buck to manage. It's really important to manage the whole season, give yourself a chance to win, and Buck is one of the best at that. There's a pride that's been restored in the Orioles. When they go play in other cities, the Orioles are considered among the best teams. They have a high-caliber team every year and they always have a chance to be there.

One of the hard parts about losing is that it's hard to stick your chest out around the rest of the country. What makes me the happiest is how everyone around the rest of the league looks at the Orioles as one of the better teams and a respected organization. That's where it all started in my mind. As someone who played for them and still watches them, I couldn't be more delighted. I think it's great for the city, great for the team.

There are a lot of gamers in baseball, guys who have grit and determination and want to win so badly. Looking at Rick Dempsey, he's exactly that. He desperately wanted to win all the time. Sometimes those intangibles are hard to find when you're looking for guys who can hit, throw, and run. Rick wanted to be in the lineup every day, he wanted to be there in crucial moments. When another team came in known for its speed and stealing bases, he loved the challenge. He thrived in saying, "Okay, I'm going to stop their running game."

It was just fun to be around him. He always wanted to do something. Being a roommate of his for three years, we didn't have any dull moments. We'd get off spring training early in the day, and he'd say, "What do you want to do today, Rooms?" And I'd go, "I don't know. I'd just as soon rest and hang out." And he'd say, "No, let's go find a boat. Let's go find this. Let's go find that." He'd always be leading you to some interesting activity or something that was fun. That was his overall personality. To have him on the team, you didn't have to worry about being a little dead coming into a game. There was life in him the whole time. And he was that way toward the end of his career, all the way into his 40s. He still had that youthful view, that joy that he brought to the game.

Rick was social; he was an extrovert. He could walk up and sing with a band and have a good time. He was a personality that Baltimore could love but also a blue-collar, hard worker. Although everyone knew he could joke around, people took him seriously because when he was on the baseball field he wanted to win. He'd get frustrated when things didn't go well. Defensively, there wasn't a catcher who could block the ball better. He was athletic coming out on bunts and throwing to second base. As a catcher he played the role perfectly. He had all the skills. And there were times when he came through offensively in a big way. We won the World Series because of him in 1983. Hitting extra-base hits, coming through in the clutch, driving in runs, he got hot at the right time.

Demper is a character. Baseball has a lot of characters, and there are some intangible values to those personalities on a team. He was definitely that and a winner as well.

—*Cal Ripken Jr.*

# INTRODUCTION

**M**y life as a baseball player covered four different decades. From my first day in September 1969 to my last day in October 1992, I took a ride that few people in this game ever experienced.

I was fortunate enough to meet and compete with many of the greatest players this game has ever known: Mickey Mantle, Joe DiMaggio, Yogi Berra, Willie Mays, Sandy Koufax, Don Drysdale, Harmon Killebrew, and Roberto Clemente, to name a few. I played for two of the most iconic teams in the big leagues, the New York Yankees and Los Angeles Dodgers. Yet I'm most proud of being known as a member of the Baltimore Orioles.

Cal Ripken, Eddie Murray, Frank Robinson, Jim Palmer, Brooks Robinson, Boog Powell. I'll stack those Orioles—along with manager Earl Weaver—against any crew from any team.

I played for George Steinbrenner, an incredibly great man. He was good for baseball because he would do anything and pay any amount to make New York the best team possible. But you know what? The Orioles always gave George and the Yankees a run for their money.

My early days in Baltimore in 1976 weren't that much fun because I got traded from the first-place Yankees to a team that was in fourth, eight games back. On top of that, I didn't get in a game that first week. When I finally got a chance to play, I got indoctrinated to The Oriole Way. Weaver, Cal Ripken Sr., third-base coach Billy Hunter, and first-base coach Jim Frey went out of their way to make sure all of us knew exactly what was expected.

That's when my career started to take off, and I realized I couldn't be in a better place than Baltimore. I had the toughest manager in baseball. We all hated Earl, day in and day out, but he brainwashed us into learning the right way to play the game. He yelled and screamed at us about mastering the fundamentals. He made us go through infield drills until we did them perfectly. After a while, you just bought into it. You knew if you could play for Earl, you could play for anyone in the world. And if he kept you in the lineup—and he did keep me in the lineup—you knew you must be doing something right.

The fans of Baltimore were a big part of the team's success. It was before the memorabilia era. The fans didn't come down to get your autograph; they just wanted to tell you how much they cared about you and the team. Wild Bill Hagy—the craziest and most loyal fan ever—and Oriole Magic will never be duplicated. It was a special time. I don't think any fans in baseball were closer to their team than ours. The Yankees had their fans, the Angels and Royals had their fans, but you just didn't see the fellowship we had in Baltimore.

I could catch any pop-up, climb up the screen if I had to, and throw out runners on the bases. I would fight anybody on the field, too. Back then, you could fight a guy and maybe get fined a couple hundred bucks, which was a lot in those days. The fans enjoyed my intensity and they appreciated the way I played the game, even though I never did reach my offensive potential. I hit .229 at Memorial Stadium and .233 over my 24-year career.

I hit far better in the minor leagues, but when I got to Baltimore, I got a lecture from Weaver, the man who loved the three-run homer. He took me to the batter's box and said, "Rick, I want you to stand close to home plate and try to drive the ball inside the left-field foul pole. That's all I care about. You do that and do your job catching the ball, and you'll play every day." Well, at the time I had great bat control and could hit to right field with ease, but Earl wanted me to do something else. So I did.

My forte became defense, mingling with the fans, and having fun playing this great game. You mix that in with all the winning we did and all the things we did as teammates, and I had the best time ever. We had enough good players; they didn't need my bat—except, perhaps, in the 1983 World Series. I'll tell you about that later.

(Baltimore Orioles)

# Chapter 1

# 1979 World Series

The Year of Oriole Magic was 1979. It seemed like we were always down in ballgames and would always come back with some miracle hit in the bottom of the ninth, two outs, and two strikes on somebody. It just seemed like fate intervened when the outcome was hanging in the balance. Sometimes, we got a clutch hit. Sometimes, the other team made an error, the roof caved in, and the Orioles came back and won the game. They started writing songs about Oriole Magic.

The 1979 Orioles were solid at the plate, in the field, and on the mound. With Eddie Murray in there, he brought another dimension. The guy would get locked in against the best pitchers in the game and hit home runs. When they made a mistake, he could hit it out to left field or right field from either side of the plate. He was just such a hard-nosed offensive player. Eddie and Doug DeCinces were really the two guys who created Oriole Magic. Eddie hit .295 with 25 homers and 99 RBIs. Doug was strong at third base and chipped in with 16 home runs and 61 RBIs.

But the guy who really put the offense together was Ken Singleton. No one talks much about Singleton, but his ability to get a walk when he wanted one was uncanny. He could take a ball a half inch off the plate with two strikes and the game on the line and get it called a ball. Umpires had a lot of confidence that he knew the strike zone. He played in 159 games that year and had 109 walks, 35 homers, and 111 RBIs. He never complained to umpires about bad calls either, and that might be why they respected him to a degree. Eddie and Singy would sit and talk hitting for hours. And you know what? I think Singy had the greatest impact on Eddie becoming a great major league player because Singy would not swing at a bad pitch if his mother's life depended on it.

Eddie was loose on the field, but he did not like the media. He didn't like them coming to him talking about a home-run streak or his batting average or the great hit that he got. He didn't want to be distracted, thinking about all the good things he had done. Today was a new day, they wiped the slate clean, and we start all over again. That was Eddie. He didn't really dislike reporters as people. He just didn't want to talk about baseball because it made him think too much about things like how many more home runs he needed to be leading the league. He didn't want those thoughts in his mind. He just wanted to go out and play baseball, focusing on each at-bat one at a time. Of course, that approach came back to haunt him later on after he retired. It was tough getting hired as a manager when you have a reputation for not being media-friendly. Then again, Eddie's changed a lot since those days.

Eddie was deathly afraid of me. We had our arguments, and I would say, "Eddie, I'm going to get you." I had a reputation for doing crazy things to people, and Eddie knew it. He had no desire to be pranked, so he would pretty much leave me alone.

Teams in those days would throw at you after you hit a home run. When they threw at Eddie, he never got angry. He got even. He just went into a concentration that we saw from the dugout, and we all said, "Thank you very much." We knew he was going to come back to get you. Eddie got a ton of big hits for us in 1979. That was the year when you started to see him become one of the best clutch hitters in the game.

Richie Dauer was another guy who got a lot of clutch hits for us. He always hit high in the order and was a good hit-and-run guy. Richie wasn't quick in the infield, but he never missed a routine ground ball to second base. He made a lot of great plays for us, too. He was as solid as they come.

Mark Belanger was still our shortstop. He broke into the big leagues with Baltimore in 1965 and was playing incredibly at shortstop 14 years later. He was a lifetime .228 hitter and batted only .167 in 1979. But he would grab a ball in the hole and then jump up and throw back to second base or first. He made plays that were inconceivable, just like DeCinces at third.

Gary Roenicke started in left field and contributed 25 home runs and 81 RBIs. He was backed up by John Lowenstein, who had a dry sense of humor, just like Mike Flanagan. Lowenstein was the one guy on the ballclub who could go to Earl during the course of a game and tell him what he should do. Oh my gosh, nobody would ever, ever think about telling Earl Weaver what he should do. Well John, he would speak up. He'd say, "You've got to send this guy up there. You've got to do this." If I had said something like that, I'd hear, "You just go back behind the plate and catch the fucking ball. Let me worry about managing the fucking team." But Lowenstein would suggest things, and Earl never contested it. And Earl would do some of those things, too. Or he would explain to John why he didn't. John was the guy who usually mimicked Earl on the bus after we won a game. Heck, Lowenstein even imitated Earl's laugh. But he only did this after we won, so Earl never did anything about it.

Dennis Martinez was a problem guy. Dennis had the best stuff I'd ever seen. I caught guys who ended up winning 16 Cy Young

Awards, and Dennis had better stuff than all of them. He was amazing when he first came up. We worked together for quite a few games. You know how Earl was: when a guy had success with a certain catcher, that was going to be the battery. But Dennis went to Earl and said, "I don't like throwing to Dempsey. He yells at me, pushes me, screams, and all that."

Dennis was experiencing quite a bit of success at the time, so Earl tried Elrod Hendricks and Dave Skaggs with him. And Dennis couldn't win any games. So Earl called us into the office the day before Dennis was pitching. He said, "Dennis, Rick Dempsey has a 42–20 record with you as a starter. That's 22 games over .500. Dempsey is going to catch you until I die. So don't ever fucking come back in this office and say anything about who you want catching you. This guy is going to fucking catch you forever. Now get out!"

That was my compliment from Earl. He let me hear that after Dennis more or less dismissed me as his catcher. Really though, Dennis never came around with us. He was 15–16 in 1979. He had a lot of issues on the field and off the field. But boy, when Dennis went to Montreal, he straightened up his life and cleaned up his act and he became the pitcher he should have been with the Orioles. He was awesome. In 11 years with Baltimore, Dennis was 108–93 with a 4.16 ERA. Not bad, but with the Expos he was 100–72 with a 3.06 ERA over eight seasons.

Scotty McGregor, I caught him with the New York Yankees in spring training, and he was a power pitcher back then. He had a 90-plus fastball, great curveball, and a solid change-up. Then he hurt his arm and came back with the Orioles as a finesse guy. He learned how to pitch, changing speeds and things like that. He was like

Jamie Moyer: slow, slower, and slowest. But Scotty could outpitch anybody. He changed his body rhythm, arm motion, worked his way through a lot of ballgames. He was incredible. Half the guys in the American League were scratching their heads after going a very nice 0-for-4, not knowing how they made all those outs.

We sent Scotty to the mound in Game 7 of the World Series in 1979. He gave up two runs in eight innings and should have gotten the W.

Sammy Stewart joined us the year before and set a record for most consecutive strikeouts for a pitcher in his major league debut. He struck out seven Chicago White Sox in a row on September 1, 1978. He only pitched in one game in the 1979 World Series, but during the 1979 regular season, he did it all. He went 8–5 with a 3.52 ERA, started three games, and picked up a save. His value to Earl was that he could start a game or finish a game, and he was pretty good at doing both.

Flanagan kind of picked up the slack for everybody, going 23–9 and winning the Cy Young Award. Flanny was very strong. He had a lot of endurance. He wanted to go deep in ballgames and never wanted to turn it over to the bullpen. This guy could throw 150 pitches and still come back out and win his next ballgame. I remember he experimented with a lot of things. He had a three-quarter delivery and every now and then he'd go to a sidearm curveball against some left-handers in tough situations. Sometimes he would pound his left foot down, stop his body rhythm, then go into slow motion, and throw the ball. It really threw hitters off. He had the hardest two-seam fastball to catch of anybody I caught with the Orioles. I turned my glove over one time to catch an inside pitch on a right-handed batter, and the ball hit me so hard

I swing during the 1979 World Series, in which I had six hits and scored three runs during my 21 at-bats. (Baltimore Orioles)

that it tore the ligament off the knuckle of my left index finger. I can still feel the hole in my knuckle where they shot it with cortisone to dissolve the bone at the end of that tendon. My God, that was a lot of pain.

\* \* \*

We started the season 3–8 and then won 15 out of 16 and starting taking over the American League. Another nine-game winning streak from June 13–23 improved our record to 47–22, and we coasted to the finish. The only AL team that had a winning record against us was the New York Yankees (6–5).

We finished 102–57 and took three of four from the California Angels in the American League Championship Series. John

Lowenstein won the opener for us with a three-run, opposite-field walk-off homer—yet another example of Oriole Magic. Unfortunately, the plot changed before we could conclude our magnificent season with a happy ending.

Coming into the 1979 Series, we were pretty confident, even though the Pittsburgh Pirates on paper were the best team in the National League. Certainly, Pittsburgh was the best offensive team in baseball. They had a lot of power with Willie Stargell and Dave Parker and Bill Robinson and Bill Madlock. Tim Foli was a good contact hitter, and Omar Moreno was an outstanding leadoff hitter.

Mike Flanagan started it off. We won 5–4, and Flanny did something you may never see again: he threw 154 pitches in a complete game. That's one thing I'll always remember.

We had Jim Palmer pitching out of the No. 2 slot. Palmer pitched well in Game 2, but we didn't score much for him in a 3–2 loss. In the first inning of the first game, we scored five runs. We didn't score anymore in that game after that and we put up only two runs in the next game. In Game 3 we got back in gear. Kiko Garcia went 4-for-4 with four RBIs, Benny Ayala contributed a home run, and we won 8–4.

In Game 4 we were down 4–0 and ended up winning 9–6 after scoring six runs in the eighth inning. At that point I thought we were going to defy the odds and win the whole thing.

As time went on after the 1979 World Series, I began to understand what happened, why we lost the final three games, and why I walked away from that season with the most disappointed feeling I ever had in the game of baseball.

I take responsibility for the ballclub losing that World Series. It was a simple remark I made to Pirates manager Chuck Tanner

I argue with the home-plate umpire during the frustrating 1979 World Series against the Pirates, who won the last three games of the seven-game series. (Baltimore Orioles)

during introductions before Game 1. We were introduced, and I came out and shook hands with everyone. Weaver was the last guy I shook hands with, and I looked over at Tanner and said, "Chuck, if you want to get this World Series over real quick, every time you get somebody on, let him try to run."

Well, he did just that. I threw out Parker in the first game and got Madlock and Matt Alexander in Game 2. Alexander was the fastest human being in the game at the time and he was there for one reason: to steal bases. I threw out those three guys, and from that game on, they just never attempted to steal a base while I was catching. That really gave them more opportunity to get some at-bats. Instead of giving away outs on the bases, they got to the plate more times.

9

That's how they kind of put their World Series back together again. Down three games to one, they started to put up the kind of runs we really expected to see from that offensive ballclub. Moreno got off to a slow start in the World Series, but he got three hits in each of the last two games and never attempted to steal off me. That gave the second hitter, Foli, the chance to get better at-bats, and he put the bat on the ball and got five hits over the last three games.

I really believe the momentum started to change after Tanner decided the Pirates weren't going to win the World Series by trying to steal bases. What he needed to do was get his team's offense on track instead of giving outs away to the catcher.

After we won the first game, Palmer did well for seven innings. But Don Stanhouse gave up a run in the ninth inning, and we lost. In that second game, I thought Earl made a huge mistake—and it showed up after it was all over. In fact, it showed up again the next year.

We came up in the bottom of the eighth inning with the score tied 2–2. Murray leads off with a single, and Doug DeCinces reaches on an error, so we have runners on first and second with Lowenstein coming up. Earl hated to bunt, but it was really the absolute perfect time to bunt. We had Billy Smith hitting after Lowenstein. Smith was a switch-hitter, and I was up after him, having a pretty good playoff and a solid World Series at that point. It would have been worth the gamble that late in the game. I mean, if it was the sixth inning, then having Lowenstein swing away would have been fine. But here in the eighth, the move itself proved to be a bad one because John hit into a double play, and Smith made the last out. Had Lowenstein been able to bunt those guys over to second and third, they would have walked Smith to get to me. If I got a hit, or someone after me got a hit, we would have won and just maybe closed it out in four straight.

So, the game stayed tied, and Pittsburgh scored in the ninth on a base hit by Manny Sanguillen to right field. It was a bang-bang play at home plate. I remember Eddie Murray cutting the ball off at first base. I would have preferred he didn't cut it off and I would have taken my chances. But Ed Ott was safe at home.

Now, go to the next year. We're playing against the Yankees in a big series. We come up in the top of the ninth with men on first and second with nobody out. Lowenstein is hitting, followed by Smith and me—again. Earl chose not to bunt, Lowenstein hits into a double play, and Smith makes the last out. The Yankees and Orioles both won 100 games, but we lost the division by three games, and that defeat sure didn't help things.

Despite that loss in Game 2 of the World Series, though, we were in great position after Game 4. We just needed one more win. Except that the roof caved in. We lost Game 5. After taking a 1–0 lead into the bottom of the sixth, we got blown out 7–1. Then the series came back to Baltimore, and we missed another chance to finish them off, losing 4–0 with Palmer on the mound.

It just seemed like everything they did worked out perfectly. We hit so many line drives that just ended up going into their gloves. The outfield was horrible at Memorial Stadium. The Colts had already played a football game on it earlier. In Game 6 Eddie hit a liner to right field, Parker slipped and fell down, and just stuck his glove up in the air, and the ball landed in it. We couldn't

Though the 1979 World Series remains a painful memory, I always will have respect for Chuck Tanner and his great Pirates team. (Baltimore Orioles)

catch a break when we got a break. We should have scored a lot more runs, but it all turned around for us—and not in a good way.

Going into the seventh game, we tried to stay positive, even though it seemed like nothing was going our way. We felt sure we could turn it all around, but all it ended up being was Willie Stargell day. He hit the home run that ended up winning the game for them. He put them up 2–1, and they won it 4–1. We were just devastated at the end of it all. It was such a depressing feeling.

Afterward, driving down the highway in Baltimore, it was just a bad, bad feeling. We just felt like we choked. That's not a good feeling in professional sports. We felt like we were going to beat any team, like we were going to be the new powerhouse in baseball beginning that season. It all appeared to be playing out that way because we had Pittsburgh on the run. They were chirping a lot, they were talking a lot, and that pissed us off. We nearly shut them up, but we didn't finish. We carried that with us until 1983.

I'll tell you, I can't listen to the song "We Are Family" at all. I hate that song, which the Pirates adopted during that season. I will always hate that song. I liked it up until the World Series, but now I'd like to break every one of those records.

We tried to recover after that, but it was tough. We had a decent season in 1980. We should have been in the playoffs in 1981, but there was a baseball strike, and they changed the rules. They decided to divide the season, and we came in second in both halves. The Yankees took a one-game lead and then they ended the first half. We finished with a better overall record than the Yankees (59–46 to 59–48), but they ended up in the World Series and we didn't even get a sniff of the postseason.

# Chapter 2
# 1983 World Series MVP

The Baltimore Orioles had a different mind-set coming to spring training in 1983. For the first time in what seemed like forever, Earl Weaver wasn't going to be there. He retired after the 1982 season, and Joe Altobelli came on the scene. Joe was 180 degrees different from Earl. Under Earl, if you walked out on the field on Day One and dropped a ball, he would be yelling and screaming at you.

Earl approached his teams from a negative sense. He would tell us we couldn't do something because he knew we wanted to prove him wrong. That's the way that team was run even before I got there. I learned about his brash ways when I was with the Minnesota Twins and I experienced it firsthand when I got to Baltimore. But the next thing you know, the Orioles are the team to beat all the time.

Getting the best of Earl, that's just how we learned to survive.

Joe was very positive. It was so unusual to come to the ballpark and find someone there who would pat you on the back and be encouraging. We didn't understand that. But it was comforting because we were all veterans by that time. We'd been through some big winning streaks, some great seasons. Joe was in our corner, and he'd let you know it. He knew we knew what we were doing. It was a whole different atmosphere and probably exactly what we needed at that time.

Earl had his principles about how to play the game. So did Joe, but he was a little more laid-back and had a far less grating personality. He was a very good manager in his own right, but we weren't used to having it so easy. We knew what to expect from Earl every day and we toed the line. But when Joe, who was a great minor league manager in the Baltimore organization, came on, it just seemed like things were so comfortable. I never had to worry about calling a bad pitch, and if we got beat in a ballgame, there wouldn't be a lot of criticism directed our way from the manager's office. It was really unnerving in a way.

\* \* \*

We were coming off a heck of a season but one that ended in bitter disappointment. We had an incredible second half in 1982. We started 2–10 and spent the entire season chasing the Milwaukee Brewers, who were really making a pretty good go at it with Robin Yount, Paul Molitor, Ben Oglivie, and big names like that. The Brewers were just a big, strong team that was making a move.

But if we were within five or six games of first place halfway through the season, we thought the division was ours. We knew we were a very good second-half ballclub. We played well at Memorial Stadium, where it was hot and always overwhelmingly humid in July and August. Teams came in and wilted while we thrived in those conditions.

We came to spring training in midseason form and only got better as the season wore on. At the All-Star break in 1982, we were 44–38. On August 27 we were 68–58, in third place, and seven games out. The next day we started a 10-game winning streak. Soon after that we swept the New York Yankees in a five-game series at home to get to 85–61 and one game out of first. As it turned out, 1982 came down to a final four-game series against the Brewers in Baltimore, beginning on October 1, and we were ready for it.

We won the first three games in blowout fashion—8–3, 7–1, and 11–3—and we went into that last game tied for first. I remember going out to dinner before that game and telling a friend, "We've really got a chance to pull this off." Oriole Magic was flourishing like you wouldn't believe.

Jim Palmer was going for us in the finale. He'd lost one game since the end of May, and we were putting a lot of runs on the board. It was Earl Weaver's last regular season game, too, so the stage was set. Don Sutton was going for the Brewers. All the armor was off, and everybody was playing for real. Yount hit two home runs, but we closed to 5–2 in the eighth inning and had runners on the corners with two outs when Joe Nolan sliced a liner down the left-field line. It would have gotten us back in the game, but Oglivie slid into that short wall in left and caught the ball. Milwaukee scored five in the ninth and won it 10–2.

It was sad that we went 94–68 (53–28 at home) and didn't go anywhere that year, but it just added to everything we were dealing with since 1979. We were embarrassed to lose the last three World Series games to Pittsburgh and then in 1982 we showed again that we were seemingly incapable of winning it all. I think everybody had that on their mind, and there was a little bit of depression that we all had. But at the end of spring training in 1983, we really had hope that we were going to put it back together again.

\* \* \*

We knew we had to get past the Milwaukee Brewers in 1983. They had Gorman Thomas, a big, strong guy. Ben Oglivie, same thing. Robin Yount was their shortstop, Paul Molitor was one of the best hitters in the game. And so on. Milwaukee was clearly one of the best teams around. The Brewers had a lot of power and a pretty good pitching staff. But we went 15–2 against them. That was a big reason why we were able to pull away so easily.

We had a decent first half, going 42–34, and at that point we pretty much knew no one was going to catch us. It came back to the notion that teams would come to Baltimore in the summer and just melt in the heat and humidity.

Even without Earl Weaver in 1983, our second-half success continued. Earl would use the first half of the season to determine what guys he was going to use in the second half. He gave everybody an opportunity, but after he identified who was an everyday player or which guy could hit a certain pitcher, that's when Earl would start platooning and using different guys in different situations. The whole first half for Earl was a learning process. Joe Altobelli became our manager by working his way up. He pretty much sent all the guys we had to the big leagues. Just about all of them played for Joe in Triple A ball, so he knew exactly who he was dealing with and how to use them.

Rich Dauer, Todd Cruz, and myself inherited a nickname from our teammates that year: the Three Stooges. I think it was Mike Flanagan who named us. Dauer was Larry, I was Moe, and Cruz was Curly. Richie, Todd, and I were fun-loving guys. We weren't afraid to make fun of ourselves in front of the ballclub. We did a lot of crazy things—in good taste. We kind of kept the team loose. At the start of a big series, it would begin with me yelling and screaming just to make the team laugh and loosen them up a little bit. Richie would always back me up with something clever to say, and Todd joined in because he was a guy who did a lot of crazy things, too.

All we wanted to do was create a looser atmosphere. We played some pretty tough teams in those days, whether it was the Kansas City Royals, the New York Yankees, or the Boston Red Sox. There was also a lot of pressure, and we hoped our antics would lighten the mood. Eddie Murray had quiet confidence, and Cal Ripken Jr. wasn't an outspoken leader either. They led more by example than talking a lot about it. We were the ones who kept everybody fired up. But we were pretty good in the field, too. Richie was at second base, and Todd was at third. They wanted to put plays on all the time just to keep things interesting. We had a secret signal where one guy would rub his wrist. Todd always looked for the opportunity to put a quick tag on somebody. We had the most fun picking guys off; we were looking for it all the time. When somebody got on base, we were all looking to see who was going to be the guy to take that one step that was going to enable me to make a pickoff play.

Richie would put his knee in front of the base and block it so the runner couldn't get back. Nowadays, they won't let you do that. Todd had such great hands; he could get rid of the ball quicker than anybody I ever saw at third base. An instant after the ball hit his glove, it was on its way to second or first base. He was incredible. We had a lot of good defensive talent out there, and they wanted to show it off all the time.

Really though, the Three Stooges were there to keep everybody smiling and keep them on their toes. We were always having fun doing something. John Lowenstein and Flanagan had the driest sense of humor, but every time they said something, the whole ballclub would stop and listen because they were so funny. They weren't at it as much as the Three Stooges, but they always got a laugh.

On and off the field, we were crazy guys who just wanted to keep the camaraderie going. The harder it got to win a ballgame, the looser we got. We made jokes about the fact that twice that season we lost seven games in a row. Despite those skids we didn't lose much ground at all. We were two games up on May 19, lost seven straight, and were still two games up. We had a two-game lead on August 5, lost seven consecutive games, and had one game shaved off our lead. When things like that happen, you begin to think that maybe this is going to be your year.

Al Bumbry was our leadoff hitter and a pretty good center fielder. He was solid on defense. He didn't have a great arm but had excellent speed and got a good jump on the ball and hit the cutoff man. Al was quiet, not an outspoken guy. He got his share of walks, but Earl wouldn't let him steal as much as he wanted to. Earl didn't believe in stealing bases that much. Al never had a green light. He didn't run much under Altobelli either. But he was our leadoff hitter that whole year, hit .275 with 31 walks, and ended up with 12 steals—two more than in 1982.

We all had a little chant before the game started. When Bumbry went up to hit, as they were announcing him, Ken Singleton would say, "C'mon Little Boomer." And everybody on the bench would go, "Ooh Ahh!" together. Wade Boggs was at third base with Boston that year. When he looked at us, everybody would point to Wade and say, "You're going to make the first error!" He heard us, and there was one time when sure enough, he made the first error. And we all went, "Ooh Ahh!" It was a stupid,

21

crazy thing. But it turned out that when Bumbry got to the plate and Singleton started his chant, Boggs would turn his back and look at center field, so he wouldn't have to see us in the dugout yelling at him. It happened for years like that.

Another character on that team was Tim Stoddard, who became the only man ever to play on an NCAA championship team and a World Series winner. The enormous pitcher was a starting forward on the 1973–74 North Carolina State basketball team that featured David Thompson. In the locker room after a baseball game, he usually had a beer in one hand and a cigarette in the other. On the field, though, he had a quiet confidence and a mean streak on the mound. If anybody messed with his team, they were going to get drilled. He'd make sure he got two outs first, and the situation had to be right, but somebody was going to get knocked down or drilled. He was 6'7" and every bit of 230 pounds—not a guy you wanted to mess with. Once he got temperamental, you would be wise to leave him alone.

Playing in his second full season in 1983, Cal was already one of the best players on the team. Cal had an energy that I had before he got there. I was getting a little bit older and starting to calm down a little bit. Cal was competitive and exuberant in everything he did. If you wanted to play tiddlywinks, Cal would find a way to beat you. He was good at ping-pong, he was good at anything you wanted to play.

He worked out 24–7 all the time, just like I did. The only difference between Cal and me is that he was a hell of a lot bigger and a lot stronger. He was just a strapping young kid who didn't even know his own strength. He loved to wrestle with the guys. He'd put you in a headlock that you couldn't escape from. At my age I was tired of getting pinned down. During spring training he watched cartoons in the morning. I wasn't even awake yet, and he would flip me off the mattress. I would fall into the corner, he would push the mattress on top of me, and then jump on the mattress. I'd be pinned between the wall and the bed, and he would sit there and watch the freaking cartoons. He would never let me up. I could barely breathe underneath that freaking mattress, and he would just laugh.

When he was in a wrestling mood, watch out. He would put you in an armlock, a leglock, a headlock, whatever. And you had to endure it for as long the television show he was watching. There was one morning in spring training when he chased me around the condo. I ran into the kitchen and went underneath the table and the chairs and I wouldn't let him get me. But Cal never knew when to stop. He would push you to the point where you wanted to fight him.

This time there was a hammer on one of the chairs. I grabbed the hammer and said, "Cal, if you get close to me, I'm going to hit you with this freaking hammer and break your toe." We roomed together for his first three years, and I'd like to think he enjoyed the experience as much as I did—well, except for the occasional submission hold.

Although our pitching was solid, we really needed one more arm to fill out the staff. A month into the season, that guy showed up. Mike Boddicker had been used sparingly in his first three seasons, 1980 through '82 but then came out of nowhere and won 16 games for us in 1983. That kid was incredible. Had he been a starter all season long, maybe he would have been the Cy Young Award winner. When he got into the rotation and started pitching as well as he did, we really got the feeling we could win the whole thing. Still, it was a strange regular season. We had some pretty good runs and a couple of really bad runs, including those two seven-game losing streaks. But nobody seemed to be able to pick up much distance on us during those times we struggled.

Joe ran a pretty good pitching staff. Along with Boddicker and Palmer, Scotty McGregor, Storm Davis, Sammy Stewart, and Tippy Martinez were all solid. We were also a good team in the clutch. We got a lot of big hits to win ballgames, pretty much the way the Orioles are playing these days under Buck Showalter. We went 98–64, and it became apparent that this was going to be our biggest opportunity to redeem ourselves for what happened in 1979.

We went into the 1983 playoffs, knowing the Chicago White Sox were going to be a really tough team to beat in this best-of-five series. They won 99 games and took the American League West by 20 games over Kansas City. We started off losing 2–1 to LaMarr Hoyt. We couldn't beat him all year. He was so tough against our lineup. We won the second game 4–0. Boddicker pitched a five-hitter, and Gary Roenicke hit a home run. Then we got to Chicago and blew them away 11–1.

In that game the White Sox started Richard Dodson. It's the first inning, and he throws an inside pitch at Murray, who was having a tough series. The thing about Eddie that everyone remembers most is that Eddie was not a fighter. He wasn't going to charge the mound or get into a scuffle with anybody for throwing at him. He was probably the toughest hitter in all of baseball to get out, the most powerful and a total clutch hitter. When they threw at Eddie, we all looked at each other and said, "Uh oh.

They're in serious trouble." Eddie got locked in, really concentrating. He was going to hurt you for trying to hit him. Sure enough, Eddie hit a three-run homer to right-center field that probably went farther than any ball we had ever seen hit at Comiskey Park.

That left us needing to win one more time to get back to the World Series.

There was a decision on White Sox manager Tony La Russa's part to either start Hoyt in Game 4 or let Britt Burns come out. He felt like he would rather go into Game 5 with Hoyt than Burns. La Russa knew he could win with Hoyt because we couldn't hit that guy. Although Burns ended up pitching an outstanding ballgame, he went into the 10$^{th}$ inning with the game scoreless and finally caved in. Tito Landrum came in as a pinch-hitter and hit the ball in the second deck to give us the lead and ultimately the win. So, La Russa did not make the right decision. You've got to win two ballgames in a best-of-five series before you can win three. Once we got past the White Sox, the World Series was ours. Everyone thought whoever won that series between us and the Sox would win the World Series, and that's how it proved to be.

Before the first game of the World Series against the Philadelphia Phillies, Dauer and I jumped up in the air, did a 360-degree turn, and then slapped our hands together. We were always thinking of things to do like that. It's not unusual for me to see all these guys doing crazy handshakes today. They've taken it to an extreme, but we had it back in our day, too. It created a lot of good chemistry on the team.

In Game 1 John Denny started for the Phillies. He was a young guy who went 19–6 with a 2.37 ERA in the National League. We were going with McGregor, who pretty much established himself as our ace going into the series. Jimmy Dwyer came up and hit a home run to put us up 1–0 in the first inning, and Joe Morgan hit one out for them to tie it in the sixth. Denny and McGregor were pitching well. Then comes the eighth inning. The start of the inning had been delayed because President Reagan did an interview that ran over the scheduled commercial time. McGregor was standing out on the mound for a long time, waiting to get going again. As the inning began, Garry Maddox stepped in and hit a home run. We couldn't come back and tie it up, Scotty lost it 2–1, and we started thinking this might not be so easy. We were up against an entire lineup of nothing but Hall of Fame players: Pete Rose, Joe Morgan, Steve Carlton, Mike Schmidt. There was a tremendous amount of talent and experience on that team.

I was walking to my car after the game and ran into Gene Michael, my old buddy with the Yankees. I said, "Man, that was a tough loss today." And he replied, "Ah, don't worry about it. You guys are going to kick their ass. You're probably going to beat them the next four games in a row." I thought, *What does he know? That's a tough lineup over there.*

\* \* \*

We got into the second ballgame, and Charlie Hudson was pitching for them. I remember it all because this was one of the biggest turning points of my entire career. It was a low-scoring game. We were down 1–0 in the fifth, and what happened next was something I hadn't done in a long time. Hudson, in fact all the Philadelphia Phillies pitchers, kept throwing the same sequence

I swing during the 1983 World Series, in which I recorded five hits, including a Game 5 home run. (Baltimore Orioles)

every time I got up. I was looking for a fastball on the outside corner, and here it came, a high one, probably out of the strike zone. I swung at this ball, making sure to go with the pitch, and I hit it to right field off the bottom half of the wall. It gave us a 2–1 lead, and we went on to win it 4–1.

As I ran around first base, it felt like a 2,000-pound weight had fallen off my back. And this is why: I was a great minor league hitter. I batted .365 before being called to the big leagues in Minnesota in 1969. In 1968 I hit .293 with 61 RBIs in 73 games and was MVP of the New York–Penn League. But Earl Weaver always wanted me to be a pull hitter. When I first got to Baltimore, he insisted that I try to take the ball toward the foul pole on the left-field line. And just like that, I lost that really good swing that I had. I just didn't go with the pitch as well. The top hand took

27

over, and my batting average dropped 100 points. That was tough. But I got a chance to play every day.

The defense is what I was there for. I had to keep that up or I would never have played in the big leagues very long. But Game 2 was a big turning point for me. Every at-bat for the rest of my career I went up there with no fear about making an out. What a difference it was, knowing that if I went 0-for-4, I didn't have to worry about not playing the next day.

In Game 3 we got down again. And of course, we kept battling to come back. I was surprised to see that they had two men on base and their manager, Paul Owens, let Steve Carlton hit with two outs in the sixth inning. I was thinking, *Oh my, this is our chance to get out of this inning without allowing any runs.* And we struck him out. They had a great opportunity to get some runs, and they let the pitcher hit. Carlton talked his way into getting to the plate. He told Owens, "I can hit this guy." He was talking about Jim Palmer, who came in as a reliever for Mike Flanagan. So Carlton told his manager he would hit a guy who was going to end up in the Hall of Fame.

In Game 4 Storm Davis started and was replaced by Sammy Stewart, who was lights out as a relief pitcher. He probably should have started that game, but we had been using him in relief, and Sammy came in and completely closed the door on them. He had such good stuff. He threw two-and-a-third innings, gave up one hit, and got us into the eighth inning before Tippy Martinez finished up.

I ended up getting pinch hit for, which was fine by me because we came back and ended up winning that game 5–4. Ken Singleton wasn't playing because we were in Philadelphia and couldn't use the designated hitter. I pretty much knew I was coming out, but getting Singleton up there was a good move. He drew a walk with the bases loaded, and that was a big run in that game. You know, Singleton was one of the big reasons why we were in the World Series in the first place. He doesn't get enough credit for what he did that year.

So now we're on the brink of winning the World Series as we go into Game 5. In the clubhouse I think everyone had a bitter memory of what happened to us in Game 5 of the 1979 World Series. And here we were with the chance to vindicate ourselves. You could hear a pin drop in that clubhouse. There wasn't anyone celebrating in advance; there wasn't music. Everybody who had experienced 1979 was sitting in front of their locker. We all knew today was the day. We were all of one thought: close the door. We weren't going to let that game go. There was a quiet and seriousness unlike any other game I've ever played in.

We had to win that game. Because if Philadelphia had won, I think everyone would be thinking that the same thing was going to happen, that it would be 1979 all over again. Scott McGregor started for us, and it turned out to be the biggest blowout of the whole World Series. McGregor tossed a five-hitter, and we won 5–0. We ended it right there.

Every single pitch was so premeditated. We knew exactly what we wanted to do with these guys. Mike Schmidt struggled the whole series and went 1-for-20. We worked him so beautifully; he just couldn't get anything going. Pete Rose got five hits, Joe Morgan went 5-for-19, but we really limited the damage with those three guys.

Anyway, we were in the third inning, and I got into a situation where I was looking for a fastball in from Hudson. I just wanted to make solid contact and I did. I hit it pretty good. It didn't go out by much. It probably scraped the back of the fence in left-center field, but it was the only home run I ever hit in postseason play. That put us up 2–0. I was just praying to God every inning from then on that the lead was going to hold up.

Well, Murray decided to come to the party that day, too. It was really funny. They put his picture on the scoreboard, and when Eddie ripped his first home run, he hit his own picture. That signified that this game was pretty much over. Then Eddie hit his second home run, gave us a 4–0 lead, and with all the firepower we had in the bullpen, we knew this game was going to go our way.

When Cal Ripken Jr. caught the line drive to end it, all that grief from 1979 was lifted. We felt so bad that we had given away that series to the Pittsburgh Pirates. It was a pretty new ballclub that had been put together in '79. I got there in '76. The next two years were decent, nothing spectacular, and then at the start of the '79 season, Weaver said, "We're going to win this thing." It was a special year, but we gave it all away. Now, finally, we were champions. After it was done, we were in the shower, and someone put soap on Flanagan's back and wrote, "Let's go home."

It was a grind playing all those years for Earl and not ever winning the World Series. We all wanted to win it in spite of him. He was a great, great manager. Even though it was hard every day coming to the ballpark, dealing with his antics and criticism, that's the way he motivated people.

We won it for Joe Altobelli, yes, and even though Joe had a really good season with us, it was still a team that Earl put together.

I embrace Scott McGregor after we won the 1983 World Series in five games. (Baltimore Orioles)

Maybe Joe was the right guy at the right time. With everybody relaxing so much, it all finally came together for us.

In 1983 I set two World Series records—including one that will probably never be beat. I tied Brooks Robinson for the most extra-base hits in a five-game World Series; I had four doubles and a home run. The second record: I was the only position player ever voted Most Valuable Player of a World Series who got pinch hit for not only once but twice.

I didn't go into the World Series thinking of being the MVP. That thought never crossed my mind. I had only played the game from the very beginning to win a championship and have a World Series ring at all costs. It was an accumulation of all the things I learned in the big leagues, beginning with my first day with the Minnesota Twins and then playing for the

New York Yankees and learning from a guy named Thurman Munson. And then coming to Baltimore and having to deal with a lot of adversity, having to play every day for Earl. Having to prove yourself to him was not a fun thing. The only way I survived it was that my father was tougher on me than Earl ever could have been. Like I told my own children, if you're going to survive in this world, the ones who make it are the ones who keep coming back, no matter how bad it gets.

That's why '83 was so special, especially after '79. We're all going to wear this ring the rest of our lives, and there was never a prouder moment in baseball for all of us who won it together. It certainly was a team effort. We never played in another World Series with the Orioles. The team started to break up after 1984 a little bit. But I took a lot of what I learned about winning baseball to the Los Angeles Dodgers in 1988, when I got my second World Series ring.

My first stint with the Orioles ended in 1986. They were going to pick up the last year of my contract and then they decided not to and brought in Mickey Tettleton to be the starting catcher. They never said anything to me about it. Just all of a sudden, I wasn't going to be an everyday player. I loved general manager Hank Peters and his entire family. But that's just the way it worked back in those days. Well, I wanted to be an everyday player and I knew I still had the talent to be one. It wasn't going to happen in Baltimore, so I said I would play for the worst team in baseball before I ever signed back with the Orioles. God was listening to me because he sent me to the Cleveland Indians. We went 61–101 that year. I played in 60 games and hit .177. Not only that, but Bo Jackson took me out on a play at the plate and broke my thumb.

That whole year, it was pretty much the opposite feeling of 1983, I'll tell you that.

* * *

My second World Series ring has a crazy story behind it. Because before the 1988 season started, I pretty much had to beg for a job with the Los Angeles Dodgers. After the 1987 season, I was looking for a job and I saw Dodgers manager Tommy Lasorda at a charity dinner. I talked to him about getting an opportunity to play for Los Angeles. I had never played on the West Coast; all my years in the league were either on the East Coast or Midwest. Being as gracious as he always is, Lasorda said, "I would love to have you. Absolutely. You've been a part of winning teams your whole career, and it would be great for us if you were a Dodger. I'll talk to [general manager] Fred Claire and get this done."

Well, I never heard from Tommy again and I never heard from Fred Claire. I didn't know if he said anything to Fred or not. So one day, I was in the garden raking leaves at my house in Los Angeles and I told myself, *Rick, you've got to go there and talk to Claire yourself. Don't depend on someone else.* I went down there at 2:00 in the afternoon, walked into the office, and asked for a meeting with Claire. His secretary said he was in a meeting, and I took a chair and waited. About an hour later, I asked the secretary if he was still in that meeting, and she said no, he was in another one. So I'm starting to get the feeling now that they're just putting me off, trying to wait me out with the hope that I'll finally just walk out the door.

After she told me three times that he was in a meeting, I just said to myself, *Okay, they're giving me the brush-off here, but I'm not leaving because I never quit at anything in my life and I'm not doing that now.* Because I know if I don't talk to him face-to-face, then it's over with for me. I waited until 7:00 PM. It was dark outside. I started to doze off a little bit and I hear the door creak open, and there's Fred at the door. I said, "Fred, just give me a few minutes of your time, and if this doesn't work out, fine. No harm, no foul. I'll get out of your life." He invited me in, and we talked for about an hour.

This was my pitch: "I know you guys lost 89 games last year. But I will hit a home run every 24 at-bats, I'll drive in a run every five at-bats. I'll take your pitching staff, and we'll turn it around. We'll win the division. And then we'll play in the World Series and we'll win it. And I'm going to catch the last pitch and give you the ball." He laughed, but I said, "I'm serious!" And he replies, "That isn't going to happen, but I like your confidence. Okay, I'm going to give you an invitation to spring training."

I platooned that spring with Mike Scioscia and had a heck of a camp. But the Dodgers also had a young catcher, Alex Trevino, who supposedly had a ton of potential. At the end of spring, Fred came to my room and asked me to go to Triple A while they decided what to do with Trevino. I just got that feeling that I was going to get worked again, so I said, "No. Fred, I've had 21 years in the big leagues. I'm 39 years old. I've had a very good career. If I don't make your ballclub, there's no hard feelings. I just appreciate the opportunity you gave me to come here and give it a last try."

At that time the great former Dodgers catcher Roy Campanella had just taken a job with the team in the community relations department, but naturally he kept an eye on what was happening on the field. I found out he asked Fred about their plans for me, and Claire said he was undecided about keeping Trevino but not going with three catchers. Campanella said it would be wrong to let me go because I was going to be able to use my experience to help the pitching staff. Fred came back and told me they let Trevino go and that I had made the ballclub.

By the end of the season, I had 167 at-bats, seven home runs, and exactly 30 RBIs. We won the division, we won the World Series, I caught the last pitch, and I was stupid enough to give Fred Claire the ball. Imagine what that ball would be worth today. But I promised it to Fred and I gave it to him.

During my brief stay with the Dodgers, I had the pleasure of witnessing one of the most memorable home runs ever hit in a World Series. Without a doubt it was the most improbable clutch home run I've ever seen in October.

Before we got to the series, we faced the New York Mets in the National League Championship Series. They beat us 10 of 11 times during the regular season. In the NLCS, though, we treated every single play as if it was the World Series and, more often than not, we did the right thing.

John Shelby was on that team and he made some incredible catches that saved us. On one particular play, a short liner into left field, Kirk Gibson ran for the ball—I don't think I've ever seen him run any faster—and he barely caught it in the web of his glove. At the same time, you could tell he hurt his hamstring. He limped off the field and didn't come back. That was in Game 7, and we won 6–0 to get into the World Series.

We were getting prepared for the Oakland Athletics, and the question on everyone's mind was: would Gibson be able to post? He was voted National League Most Valuable Player that year, even though he only had 76 RBIs. But it seemed like every one of them was a game-changer or a game-winner. It would have been devastating not to have him in the World Series. But if he couldn't make it, well, we would just have to count on one of our no-name guys—Danny Heep, Franklin Stubbs, Dave Anderson, Jose Gonzalez. No one knew who the hell they were, but they could play. Heck, half the team was a bunch of platoon players, backup guys, and old, washed-up guys like Mickey Hatcher and myself. Okay, maybe not completely washed-up. Hatcher batted .368 and hit two home runs in that series.

So we go into that first game and we knew we weren't going to have Gibson. He could barely walk to the plate and wasn't even a part of the introductions because it would have been too painful for him to walk from the dugout to the baseline. We're at home with the National League rules of no designated hitter, so Gibby wasn't going to play. And although we got two runs in the first inning, Jose Canseco hit a grand slam in the second inning to make it a 4–2 game. We battled back to 4–3 in the ninth before Mike Davis came up with two outs against Dennis Eckersley. He worked the count for a walk. When he walked there was really no one left on the bench. Lasorda was looking for somebody to pinch hit. Gibson was taking some swings in the clubhouse and he had someone give a message to Lasorda that he could do it. So Tommy said, "Okay, let's go."

I'm standing on the rail, and Gibby limps out to the warm-up circle. I'll never forget it. He could barely get himself into the batter's box. I said out loud, "How's this guy going to be able to do anything?" It turned out to be one of the most incredible at-bats you'd ever want to see. The first pitch was fouled off, and Gibson limped out of the box looking like a 100-year-old man. You could tell he couldn't get around on the fastball. Then he hits a chopper down the first-base line, and Gibby hobbled to first just in case it stayed fair. He couldn't even run as far as the ball did. Eckersley was about to pick it up just before it rolled foul.

Eckersley tries to get Gibby to go fishing by throwing the ball outside, and Kirk isn't biting. Three straight balls go outside, and now it's a full count. One thing we had on our scouting report was that Eckersley always—100 percent of the time—threw the slider outside and away on left-handed hitters when the count was 3–2. So we were looking for it. Davis had stolen second, so we didn't need a home run. All we needed was a base hit to extend the game.

So Eckersley throws the slider away, just as we all expected, and there it goes. I don't know how Gibby did it because it didn't look like a home-run swing. But his hands went out after the ball, and he made good, solid contact. Off the bat, that ball was gone. We were so freaking amazed—he was halfway down the first-base line and we were already on the field. It was incredible to watch him go around the bases, pumping his arm. Lasorda, I thought he was going to have a heart attack, moving that big body like he did. Dodger Stadium was on fire. Everyone was standing, everyone was cheering. It was one of the most amazing home runs in baseball history.

After recording five extra-base hits, I received the 1983 World Series MVP, though I joke that I'm the only MVP to also get pinch hit for twice. (Baltimore Orioles)

That World Series was David against Goliath. Our slingshot was Orel Hershiser. He was the equalizer. This guy could beat any team that year. He had the most amazing sinker, one that moved better than any I had ever caught before. He had Jim Palmer-like control and he just knew what he was doing. This series, however, will be remembered for Gibson's home run. That, by the way, was his only at-bat in those five games. I'm proud of being a part of that team. But that ring is at home. The World Series ring I got in 1983, well, that's never leaving my finger.

# Chapter 3

# From Bank Robbers to the Bronx Zoo

**W**hen I first started thinking about playing baseball, I had a cousin, Dick Young Jr. His father was a World Boxing Hall of Fame referee, who worked fights involving Muhammad Ali, Ken Norton, and Emile Griffith. Boxing goes deep in our family, just like baseball. I was related to Jack Dempsey; he was my grandfather's cousin. My father was an opera singer and did a play on Broadway called *The Song of Norway* and he played a character named Rikard. That's how I got my middle name. I'm John Rikard Dempsey, but I was born in Fayetteville, Tennessee, and southerners are always called by their middle name. So, I was Rick Dempsey.

If I had idols growing up, they were my cousins, Bill and Dick. They used to umpire my Little League games, and whenever I made an out, I would cry. Dick went on to sign professionally out of high school and went on to play in the Cleveland Indians organization. That's when I started thinking about catching. Unfortunately, while he was warming guys up in the bullpen, he got a bone bruise on his hand. The padding on catcher's mitts in those days was just too damn thin. It eventually ended up costing him his career.

My brother, Pat, is seven years younger than I am and four inches taller. He got into baseball just like I did. He wanted to follow in my footsteps. We talked baseball and practiced together all the time. He spent 13 years in the minor leagues but got to drinking a little bit too much and did some recreational stuff, and it ended up ruining his career. He could have been an outstanding catcher, but his off-the-field habits caught up to him. He had to spend two years in the John Lucas Wellness and Aftercare Program, a substance abuse recovery program. He did not want to come out until he knew he could handle life without drinking. He's in his 60s now and a four-time long drive champion in golf. He can hit a golf ball about nine miles and was voted into the Long Drive Hall of Fame. I couldn't be more proud of the way he turned his life around.

My son, John, played professionally for five years. He was picked in the 10th round of the 1989 amateur draft by the St. Louis Cardinals. He was a switch-hitting catcher, a left-handed hitter who learned to hit right-handed, too. I was still playing when he got in the game. He had a completely different personality from me, which isn't a bad thing. I tried to work with him, but I think I pushed him hard. I regret not being able to relate to him because he might have done better with a different instructor. I learned later from my own experiences that I needed to be a better coach with my own son. He's a very smart kid and he came to me after five years in the minors and said, "Dad, I want to go back to college." I couldn't have been happier because he was spinning his wheels in the Cardinals organization. He said, "Dad, I don't want to be 27 years old and finish my career and have nothing to fall back on." I sent him to Villanova, and he loved it there. He got a finance degree and now he's very sought after in California. He's a finance guy, working for a big company.

Gregg Zaun is my nephew and he ended up having a fine career in the big leagues. We used to work on a few things when he was younger. He was already a good catcher. He spent hours working with my brother, Pat, who gets the credit for making him a very good major league receiver. Gregg set up well. He didn't have a great arm, but he did a pretty good job throwing. He was better at handling a pitching staff. That was one of his strengths.

My dad was a swimming pool contractor after his short tenure as an opera singer on Broadway. He went out to California and got into the construction business. He bought a nice house in

Woodland Hills, California, a big Spanish hacienda. It had a long driveway down to Mulholland Drive.

He allowed the city to build a Little League field at the end of our driveway on a large piece of land. When my father wanted to punish me for not doing my chores or whatever, he would forbid me to go to the field. But I loved baseball so much that I would wait until he would leave for work and sneak down the stairway on the back of my balcony, run through a special little secret trail that I had to the ballpark, and spend all day playing baseball. If there were teams playing there, I would make them let me join in. Sometimes I would take those baseballs that they fouled off into the gullies and hide them and keep them for myself.

That's where my love for the game of baseball began—even if it meant standing up to my father, who was 6'4", 260 pounds with hands three times the size of mine. If you got in trouble, he wouldn't be afraid to knock you around a little bit. But he was a great guy and probably brought the energy of the game out in me as I played Little League.

I was always part of the All-Star team, and we started to develop quite a team of future stars. The team actually played on my property. Then we went up to Pony League, and I was the last kid to be voted to the Canoga Park-Woodland Hills Pony League All-Stars, which had eight players who ended up signing professional contracts. And that doesn't count Hall of Famer Robin Yount, who was the batboy. We won 12 tournaments to become the West Coast representatives in the Pony League All-Star tournament in Pennsylvania at Washington-Jefferson College in 1963. It was just a massively talented All-Star team.

What we didn't realize at the time was that in Los Angeles there were a lot of banks being robbed. Back then, bank robbers were kind of idolized to the point where they got nicknames all the time. There was one pair called "The Mutt and Jeff Bank Robbers," a big, tall guy and a short guy. Turns out, the manager of our team, John Jennings, was the tall guy. We never did see the short guy.

Jennings got arrested after our 13th tournament. He robbed a bank in a Pennsylvania city where everybody knows everybody. He was identified by a lady who saw his picture in their little newspaper there during the tournament. She said, "That's the man that hit me coming out of the bank." FBI agents, Van Nuys (California) detectives, and officers from the Central Division Robbery team found Jennings counting the cash. He had an insurance business back then, too, but nobody ever knew that while we were winning baseball games he was robbing banks, hustling to the ballpark, changing into his managerial uniform, and working the game as the police cars went flying by.

Our shortstop was Terry Hankins. His father was a police chief in Los Angeles assigned to the case of the Mutt and Jeff robbers. He never knew the guy he was looking for was the manager of his kid's All-Star team. Jennings, who smoked a cigar all the time, went to prison and he died of tongue cancer. He died while he was watching me become the Most Valuable Player of the 1983 World Series.

\* \* \*

Out of all the great teams I played for and all the people I met in the game, one of the most meaningful moments of my career was getting to know Harmon Killebrew when I got to the big leagues for the first time with the Minnesota Twins. He was the only major league player who would even say hello to me when I showed up in September of 1969 to play my first major league game. In those days players wouldn't even talk to you. The only guys who introduced themselves were guys in the same boat as you like Eric Soderholm. Rod Carew and most of the other established major league guys wouldn't even look at you. You couldn't even walk across their position. You'd even have to walk around them to shag fly balls.

I can remember that first September that I spent with the ballclub at 19 years old. They made us go to the bat rack and get the old bats that players didn't use anymore. I picked out a Carew bat, not knowing that he was the greatest hitter in the game. (He ended up with seven batting titles.) As kind of an initiation, Rod would come in, take the bat out of your hand, and say, "Don't ever touch one of my bats again."

Then Killebrew gave me this advice: you've got to stand up to these guys. Make them respect you, or it will happen again. So it happened a second time, and I kind of got into a confrontation with Rod. I said, "Don't come around to get that bat a second time. I know the routine." He looked at me kind of funny, sort of like, *Is this kid serious?*

I started playing winter ball in 1969 in Aragua, Venezuela, the city where Carew was raised. We'd go down there because if you didn't get 250 at-bats at the major league level you were eligible to play winter ball. I needed the at-bats to become a better big league player. From the very beginning, as soon as you got off the airplane in Venezuela, you'd see a lot of military personnel. We were driving through the mountains and saw soldiers walking alongside the road. They were under martial law at that time. I played in Venezuela from 1969 through 1974 and, let me tell you, I have memories of that place that will last a lifetime. We had some wild times down there.

My hotel in Aragua had a beautiful view and a fantastic swimming pool. It was pretty damn hot, so I jumped into the shallow end of the pool. I'm looking around, and there were all sorts of people milling around. I was getting comfortable in my surroundings when out of the corner of my eye I saw this green thing coming right at me. It was an iguana, but to me it was the biggest lizard in the world. It was headed my way and didn't seem to care one bit that I was in the water. Turns out, the waiters there would catch iguanas, cut their stomachs open, take the eggs out, and eat them. It was a delicacy. Well, a waiter was chasing this lizard, which had no intention of being someone's lunch. It had to be around four feet long. It jumped right into the swimming pool, and just as quickly, I jumped out. It went to the bottom and just stayed there. I didn't spend much time in the pool after that.

What an eye-opener it was that first year, seeing what another country was all about. You had to watch your Ps and Qs or you could get in trouble. Enos Cabell, a very good hitter and an outspoken guy, was a young kid in the Orioles organization. Toward the end of the 1969 season in winter ball, we lost early in the playoffs and were eager to get back home. In order to get out of the country, you needed a certificate to prove you did your work and paid your taxes.

We got the paperwork we needed, but our plane wasn't leaving until the next day. We were lounging around the hotel, and one of the country's famous boxers walked into the lobby accompanied by a lovely lady and a bunch of bodyguards. She went over to get a coffee, and Enos said something to her. I don't know if he was coming on to her or what, but she got very offended. The boxer came to her defense, and he and Enos got into a shoving match. It escalated, and Enos slugged one of the boxer's bodyguards. The woman took an ashtray and slammed it over Enos' head. He turned around and took a swing at her. It was total chaos.

As they attended to the bodyguard and the girl, we knew what we had to do. The police were going to come and put us in jail. This was one of the country's national heroes, and Cabell got into a fight with his entourage and punched his girlfriend. We figured they'd arrest all of us and throw us in jail, so we started hustling to get out of there. Enos started yelling, "We've got to get out of here! Pack up your stuff and let's get to the airport. Let's get out of here so we don't have to stay all winter. We'll find someplace to fly to." So we all threw our shit in a bag and got in a cab on our way out. We headed to the airport in Caracas. We got there, and the only flight out was to the Bahamas. We got on that flight and took off just before the police cars arrived. We spent the night there and took a flight to New York. One of the American players involved wasn't so lucky. He got arrested at the hotel and was stuck in Venezuela for another month.

I played two years in Aragua and the third year I played in Caracas. That was an incredible city. There was someone there who looked like Buster Brown, a little guy with red hair. He was head of the secret police. He was known there as *El Turco*, or "The

Turk." He was a big fan of the Caracas team there. This guy ran the damn country. He was the Earl Weaver of police. He was the meanest guy. Back then, groups of Communists gathered in Caracas and had secret meetings. El Turco would get wind of it, bring three of his guys loaded with pistols, and break it up.

Well, we were playing a game there, and I got plunked by a pitch. I charged the mound and got into a fight. Bam, bam, bam, I hit the pitcher three times, and the fans started going nuts. Baseball down there, you've never seen anything like it. They light fires in the grandstands when their team isn't winning and they gamble like crazy. The stands are packed every single game. Baseball was the biggest thing in the country. So on this night, I got thrown out of the game, and people were mad at me for slugging the local star pitcher. They were even peeing in cups and throwing them at me. Finally, the game was over, and we had to go to the parking lot to grab a cab and get back to the hotel. A couple of the guys got in one cab, and I ran through the parking lot to get into another. There were thousands of people out there leaving the game, and all of a sudden some guy saw me and yelled my name. He ran at me and kicked me in the back. I turned around and started hitting him. I got him on the ground, and the fans started circling around us. This guy was kicking at me, and I was pelting him with punches. He finally had enough, and I jumped in the cab. That's when all those fans swarmed around the cab.

The cab driver had the doors locked, and he was screaming at the fans in Spanish while they rocked the cab back and forth. They were going to flip it over, and I was scared to death. There were so many people, you couldn't even see light out of that car. All of a sudden, everybody came to a complete stop. They started to part like the Red Sea for Moses, and I'm thinking, *What the fuck is happening here?* Here comes El Turco. The little son of a bitch had his gun in his hand and four of his henchmen with him. Nobody fucks with El Turco. All of a sudden, a few of my teammates rushed up and got in the cab. Bo Diaz, a catcher in the Boston Red Sox organization, was in the front seat. I was in the back with two other Latin players. Now he got the cab moving, and all of a sudden, that little guy I punched out threw a brick at the car. It went right through the window and hit Diaz in the neck. He was bleeding badly, the cab driver had glass in his eyes, and the car was a mess. Diaz was screaming as the blood was gushing. I took the padding out of my catcher's mitt and put it on his neck. I said, "You've got to get this guy to the hospital right now before he bleeds to death!" The cabbie took off, drove on the wrong side of the street, and got us to the hospital.

Back then, the police carried long sabers. As we took Diaz into the hospital room, the police came with their sabers drawn. I ran out the back of the operating room, but they had two more guys waiting for me. They handcuffed me and took me to jail. When I got there, they had the guy who threw the brick handcuffed to one of the jail cell bars. I got handcuffed to a cell bar, too. I was within kicking range of the asshole, and boy, did I start kicking at him. I was still wearing my spikes! He was screaming in Spanish, and the police started screaming at me in Spanish, and, of course, I had no idea what they were saying. It was a madhouse, and then all of a sudden, it got completely silent. Yep, here comes El Turco. He said a few words to them, and then a policeman came over and took off my handcuffs. They took me out and back to the hotel.

Vic Davalillo was my roommate. He grew up in Venezuela and was playing with the Cleveland Indians at the time. We had an early morning flight the next day for a game in some other city. Vic wasn't there, so I figured he was out drinking because he did that just about every night. I was lying there in my bed, trying to rehash in my mind what happened that crazy night. I was a nervous wreck because I didn't know what was going to happen next. Was someone going to come into the hotel and try to assassinate me? Who knew? Well, Vic came in the room, and then I felt something next to me in bed. It was Vic. He said, "Hey, roomie!" And then he passed out. So I climbed over him and went to sleep in his bed. Then we woke up early and got ready to play. God bless him, Vic Davalillo could hit the baseball whether he was sober, drunk, or hung over.

El Turco was a big fan of Leones del Caracas, the local team in the Venezuelan Professional Baseball League. He would go down on the field during the games. Crowds parted when he walked by because he was head of security. Everybody knew of him. One day, he was going to take us to a racetrack. I had never seen horse racing, so this was going to be a first for me. Pete Koegel, a utility man with the Milwaukee Brewers, Pete Mackanin—now the manager of the Philadelphia Phillies—and I were in the car with El Turco and his guys. On the way there, he got orders to stop by this Communist meeting right in the middle of the city. He told us, "You boys wait here while I talk to these guys." He took his guys with him. Well, we wanted to see what was going on, so we looked through the window. El Turco walked in and cut right in the middle of 15 or 20 people in there talking. He said something, they started yelling at him, and he pointed his gun at one of the Communists. The guy says, "Ah, fuck you." And he shot the guy right there. We all look at each other, and I said, "What the fuck did we just see? El Turco blasted this guy!" Everybody started throwing chairs and stuff, and we took off. You talk about an eye-opener. We got the hell out of there, grabbed a cab, and went back home. We never found out what happened to El Turco after that. We never saw him the rest of the season.

One of the neat things about Caracas was that fireworks were completely legal, and they would sell these huge rockets on the street. They were at least three feet long and had like a quarter stick of dynamite at the end. People would shoot them in the air around Christmas. We got a bushel of them. I accidently lit one in the car, and it shot out the window and into the car next to us, a little Volkswagen. You could see the whole car was full of smoke, and all of a sudden, the back window blew out. The guy got out of his car and had no idea what just happened. Thank God we didn't kill the poor bastard.

Later, we got on top of our hotel, where you could see the whole city. You light one of these things, it burns all the hair off your arm before it took off. The rocket would go a quarter of a mile before it started to come down. We could see security guys three or four blocks away, across the Sabana Grande freeway. We were firing those rockets off, and one of them chased a guard underneath a parking hangar. Another one hit a house and blew the screen door right off its hinges. We were out of control, but heck, we were just young guys having some fun.

Paul Casanova was a big star catcher with the Atlanta Braves. He played for the Sharks La Guaira, and we played for Caracas, but we all lived together in the city because the teams were close to each other. It would be like the Bronx and Manhattan. We helped him build his bar and then drank there quite a bit. Pete LaCock— the son of *Hollywood Squares* host Peter Marshall—Mackanin, and I went to his bar a few blocks from the hotel one night. Mackanin was talking to this girl. The locals got pissed off because it was some guy's girlfriend. We decided to go home, but Mackanin stayed for another minute or two. We started walking down the freeway, and all of a sudden Mackanin ran out of the bar and yelled, "Let's get the fuck out of here!" Turns out, he got into a scuffle with a couple of the guys, and they pulled a gun on him. Pete couldn't figure out what to do, so he jumped on this wall as the bullets were fly- ing. He jumped off the wall and onto the roof of a house. He fell through the ceiling into the living room. We ran back to the hotel, and about 20 minutes later, Mackanin showed up. He was cut up and bleeding, but it was still better than getting hit by a bullet. He said, "I couldn't find the door! It was dark, and I kept stepping on people. I was lucky as hell to get out alive!"

I liked to go to some of the beaches in Venezuela when we got an occasional day off. One day during winter ball in 1971, I took a ride to a beach with LaCock and Ed Sprague, a pitcher with the Oakland Athletics. It was a beautiful inlet near Puerto Cabello. But it was where Herman Hill, an outfielder with the Twins, drowned in December 1970. He went into the water and got sucked out because the bottom of the sea there was full of peb- bles, not sand, and it was hard to get your footing. It would give way under your feet. He got caught in a current and panicked and drowned.

It felt good to walk on those pebbles, but big waves came into the inlet. I remember how difficult it was to swim there. It scared the shit out of me when I got sucked out. The wave would bring you back, but it was dangerous and deadly if you panicked. Pete and I went out and had to scramble to get back to shore. I crawled onto some jagged rocks, tried to grab hold, and a wave hit me. I got cut to shreds and lost my wedding ring. Those were weird, crazy times in Venezuela, no doubt about it.

* * *

I was traded from the Minnesota Twins to the New York Yankees in October of 1972. I didn't want to leave Billy Martin; I thought he was the greatest manager that I had ever seen, but I got traded for Danny Walton. Minnesota wanted a left-handed hitting catcher. I was a right-handed hitting catcher, so I went to back up Thurman Munson. As it turned out, it wasn't the last I saw of Billy Martin.

When I first walked into Yankee Stadium and saw all the history and nostalgia of the place, it was incredible. You think about Babe Ruth and Mickey Mantle and all of the great players who played there. I got a chance to meet Elston Howard and players of that caliber. Yogi Berra was still coming to spring training along with Mickey Mantle that first year. Oh my God, you talk about going to heaven in a baseball sense, that's what it was.

And the Yankees fans were like nobody I'd ever met at that point. They knew who I was two weeks into the season. I was walking down the street in the Bronx, and a cab driver was yelling, "Hey, Rick Dempsey! Welcome to the Yankees! You look like a helluva ballplayer. Good luck to ya!" Then someone else walked down the street and said just about the same thing. Amazing.

It was a lot of fun. But trying to get some playing time there was almost impossible because Munson was great. If I could say I ever had an idol in the game, it was him. He was such a hard-nosed player, and everyone in the clubhouse loved to rally behind him. He just stuck his face in it every single day. Although I was probably a better defensive catcher than he was at the time, it just never dawned on me that there was any kind of a comparison at all in anything. I talked to him incessantly about how to handle pitchers and learn the things I needed to do to be just like him.

Thurman took me under his wing immediately and so did Sparky Lyle and Catfish Hunter and Bobby Murcer. Those guys just kind of embraced me. I thought it was going to be tough to make it and get exposure, but it was actually the opposite. They immediately gave me a job with the ballclub; it was part of the inner-team structure. I had the title of the Grand Poobah. I was the one who made sure to know where the parties were going to be, and anytime they needed anything done that they didn't want the organization to know about, then I was the guy who had to get that done ahead of time. It wasn't anything too crazy or anything that involved drugs.

Well, there was one exception. We had card games all the time. There was one time I won $50 or $60 and decided I was going to buy a new pair of Florsheim shoes. I was pretty proud of those darn shoes, and that night we all went to a party in Texas. Some of the people there were smoking dope. That was something none of us ever did. But we're in that room with a bunch of high-rolling New York people, and I'm talking with Thurman and Bobby. Just smelling the smoke started to make me really hungry. I'm thinking, *This is a funny feeling. What's going on here?*

So I decided to go to the candy machine down the hallway. I walked out the door and I couldn't feel my feet. Anyway, I needed to get some change for the candy machine because I was starving. I put my feet on the ground and started shuffling forward because I didn't think I could walk without tipping over. I didn't want anyone to think I was drunk or stoned or anything like that. I shuffled my feet through the parking lot to the front desk, got some change, and came back. I bought everything— Jujubes, Smarties, Good & Plenty. I was eating everything. Finally I got sick. I got over the toilet seat and vomited out everything. As I laid back against the tub with my legs crossed, I looked down at my brand new Florsheim shoes and they had no leather on the bottom of them! One day old, and they were ruined from shuffling my feet. I got high from just smelling the smoke.

On the field Catfish was the biggest pitcher in the game of baseball at that time and he really attached himself to me because the first couple of games he won that season were with me warming him up. Then I had to be there every day he pitched. He used to make a circle on top of the ball before he took his first warmup pitch. He said, "Rick, I want you to spit in that circle." He was a country boy all the way. So I said okay and I hocked a big loogie right on the top of the ball, and he rubbed it in for good luck and then started his warmup.

He kept on winning, so every time he pitched, I had to make sure I was in the bullpen on time and had to make sure I spit on that ball. He was superstitious about it. He said, "You'd better be there on time and you'd better be ready to spit on that ball." He wouldn't throw to anyone else.

Gene Michael was a shortstop, a platoon guy. He also took me under his wing. He was one of the best guys I ever met in baseball. He was the prankster on the team. All the good players looked up to him because he was an old pro. He knew how to handle himself in New York and on a winning ballclub. He used to get on certain players who had elite status. He didn't have that status, but he still made them respect him. And they learned the game from him.

But he wasn't immune from our pranks. I remember one spring training we were going to have a team meeting and I put a mouse in the cup of his jockstrap. Thurman put me up to it. I just had to do it because that was my job—to do all the extra stuff. Before the meeting everyone knew it was there. The mouse was in his cup, and it curled up and went to sleep because it was nice and warm in there.

Gene went and put his pants on, and we're all watching him put his Yankee uniform on. Billy started to talk, and Gene was sitting back. He didn't feel it yet. I can remember Graig Nettles walked by, and he had a bat in his hand and he tapped Gene on the cup. It looked like it was nothing more than a fresh little gesture, but then all of a sudden that mouse woke up.

So Gene started jumping around, yelling, and he couldn't get out of those pants fast enough. He tore them halfway down, he felt the mouse, and he tore at it, and all of a sudden he caught his spikes on his sock, and he tore the sock. He was bleeding and trying to rip the jock off. He finally got it off, and everyone was in hysterics. That mouse came out of the jock and staggered across the floor. It looked like he had been drinking for three nights.

I loved being around Billy. As long as you gave Billy 100 percent, there was never any issue, never any problems. At the beginning there was really no issue because he was winning. Soon, however, when George Steinbrenner wanted him to get rid of certain players, Billy started to protest. The way baseball was in those days, owners didn't get involved and didn't tell managers what to do, especially managers like Billy Martin.

I liked George. Not many players liked George at first, but whenever he was around the little people on the team—like myself—he treated us right. He'd say, "Listen, I want you to go to my restaurant in Cleveland, and everything's going to be covered." He was always taking care of the players, and I appreciated it because being able to save your meal money was a big thing back in those days. If you got in a ballgame and got a hit, George never forgot it. If you did something good in a ballgame, George would always say something about it.

In 1974 we were having a good year, and with two games left, we still had a chance to beat the Orioles for first place. We won the series in Cleveland and were on to Milwaukee. One of the guys on the team that year was named Bill Sudakis. He was always very outspoken and talking about how he was from Chicago and how tough he was, that kind of thing.

Murcer and Munson were on the plane and they were teasing him about being the third-string catcher and not the second-string catcher. Bill got really upset with them, and said, "Well, who's the second-string catcher if I'm not?" And they said, "Dempsey is." Well, instead of taking it out on Thurman and Bobby, he saw me sitting down the aisle and started walking toward me. Now, this was a commercial flight with regular people in the back half of the airplane.

He took my sandwich, took a bite out of it, and threw it back on my dish. I said, "Bill, what are you doing?" He said, "I don't like you." I guess he had a little bit to drink. So all of a sudden, he took a fork off my tray and stabbed me in the chest. It went through my jacket and stuck in my chest. I said, "What in Sam Hell are you doing?" I knew that was enough to start a fight, but I wasn't going to do anything on an airplane. I was all of 5'11", 170 pounds at the time. I kept my composure, and Bobby and Thurman got Bill to sit down. But for some reason, Bill wouldn't let it go. At this point, I was bleeding in the middle of my chest. We got off the airplane and got on the bus, and he spent the whole ride just verbally harassing me. He wanted a fight.

I knew something was going to happen, but it wasn't going to be on the airplane or the bus. So as soon as the bus pulled into the Pfister Hotel in Milwaukee, I ran off the back of the bus and into the hotel. I threw my suitcase in a corner and stood right in the middle of the lobby and waited for him to come off the bus. Well, Murcer came by, grabbed me by the elbow, and said, "Demps, you gotta let it go, big series. Go on up to your room and let it go."

But Bill grabbed me by the other arm and swung me around. And he said, "What's it going to be, you little chicken shit? Street fighting or boxing gloves? Which way you wanna do it?" I said, "Neither!" and hit him three times, knocked him out cold. Then I started to hit anybody near me because I knew he wasn't going to be down for long. I wanted to go over and finish him off. My roommate, Dave Pagan, grabbed me. I knocked him over a glass table and broke it. Now everybody's starting to panic. "No Neck" Williams tried to jump me. Murcer was holding me from behind and he fell to the floor, and I stepped on his hand and broke his finger, though I didn't realize it at the time.

I was swinging at everybody until it got to the point where I couldn't lift my arms up anymore. Thurman grabbed me from behind, started to choke me, and I passed out. So now I was done. Bill was on his feet again; he reached in while everybody got a hold of me and grabbed me by the sweater and tore my shirt off. They finally got Bill subdued, and I couldn't even walk. Elston and Thurman pulled me into a side bar and gave me a shot of whiskey to calm me down. It took me about a half hour to recover, and finally I went up to my room.

Bill Virdon was the manager that year, and he said if anyone threw another punch it was going to be a $2,000 fine. That's like getting fined $100,000 today. So that was that. But Sudakis was a little embarrassed that I got the best of him, so he swore at the end of the season he was going to kill me. Well, I have an Uncle Sonny who was the head of the Yonkers racetrack for a while. I lived with him while I was a Yankee. He was connected to some people who…he never said and I didn't ask, if you catch my drift. When they closed the Yonkers racetrack, he was the main guy at the Meadowlands. He knew a lot of shady people, and everybody knew I was his nephew. They would tell Sonny, "Hey, ya know, we really like your nephew. He's a hell of a player and has a Yankee heart. We don't like this guy, Bill Sudakis."

So, I got a phone call. Some guy with a gruff voice I didn't recognize said: "Hey, Rick Dempsey, don't worry about that guy Sudakis. We're going to take care of him for you. You just keep playing good ball and don't worry 'bout nothing." Then he hung up the phone.

I called up my Uncle Sonny and said, "Please don't let your boys do anything! I'll figure this out. It's just a baseball fight." My

Uncle Sonny never admitted he made a call to his buddies, but he probably did.

That wasn't the end of it, though. Steinbrenner called us both into the office. Sudakis went first. He released Bill right away. I had tears in my eyes, knowing I was going to be released as a New York Yankee on account of all this. I didn't mean for it to happen, but it happened. We lost one game in that series on a fly ball to right center that Lou Piniella couldn't catch, and Bobby Murcer probably would have.

Steinbrenner called me in, and I knew I was in for it. He said, "Rick, I'm not too happy about what went on at the Pfister, that we lost Bobby and lost the championship. I just want you to know one thing: I'm very proud of you. Thurman and Bobby told me what happened, so it's all right. I don't want you to worry about it." I'm thinking, *George Steinbrenner's telling me it's okay?*

George and I became good friends at that point, even though he did trade me away to the Orioles on June 15, 1976, in a 10-player deal. But he never held that fight against me, and every time I saw him we talked about that day. I think George always kind of liked that kind of thing. Although some people didn't like him because he was very outspoken, did things his way, and would repeatedly fire Billy, I loved him.

# Chapter 4

# The Earl of Baltimore

When I was in my early days with the Minnesota Twins, Bob Allison and Harmon Killebrew talked about this guy, Earl Weaver, all the time. I remember playing a game against the Orioles. I met Boog Powell and Brooks Robinson while they were playing catch in front of the stands at Memorial Stadium. They told me about Earl and his notorious antics, how he was always yelling and screaming with the umpires and going crazy. I thought it was a little strange because I always had the ultimate respect for authority. My parents beat that into me.

So it was kind of funny that I ended up being traded to the Orioles in June of 1976. I joined them in Chicago while they were playing the White Sox, and Earl told me starting catcher Dave Duncan was playing very well. He said, "Dave's hitting the ball solidly for us right now, but when I get a chance to put you in the game, I'll do it."

We had six games left on that road trip, and I never played once.

I just came from the New York Yankees, and they were in first place by five and a half games. I was looking forward to getting into the playoffs with New York and getting my first World Series ring. We were that good. So it was so depressing, so disappointing to get traded and then not even get into a ballgame for more than a week.

I'll never forget that first night I got to Baltimore. They dropped us off from a bus at the Best Western Hotel at the corner of York Road and I-695. It was one of those nights where it was 90-some degrees with 96 percent humidity. They didn't have rollers on suitcases back then, and I had three big suitcases—plus a hang-up bag. We went to the front desk, and I got my key. My room was in a bungalow across the parking lot and on the second floor. Once I got up there, dragging a ton of luggage to the end of the hall, I stuck the key in the door, and it didn't work.

That was the straw that broke the camel's back for me. I hadn't played since the trade, I was hot, tired, pissed off, and had all that damn luggage. I threw all of it over the rail onto the parking lot. The suitcases busted open; clothes went everywhere. I sat on the top step crying, thinking, *Is this what my career has come to?* Not only was I not with the Yankees anymore, which really broke my heart at the time, but I thought I was going to be out of baseball soon.

I cleaned everything up, got my key, and went to the room. Turns out, Orioles general manager Hank Peters had gone up to Earl and said, "You've gotta play this guy. You've got to give him a chance."

I stayed on the bench for the first game of the homestand against the Boston Red Sox and then finally made my Orioles debut as a starter on June 22. It was exactly a week after the trade. I went 0-for-3, and we lost 6–5 in 15 innings. It was not exactly a memorable event. I left for a pinch-hitter, and Duncan finished up.

I got the first of my 854 hits with the Orioles when I next played on June 26. For the record it was a double against the Cleveland Indians. I didn't do much at the plate early in my career with Baltimore, but I proved I was solid defensively. I was building a solid rapport with the pitching staff and kept base stealing to a minimum. There was no way to overlook my contribution to the team. Not that I heard anything from the manager.

Earl would never pat you on the back and say you had a good night. He would never say, "Nice hit." Nothing. He didn't want

Whether on the mound or in pregame meetings, I always found Earl Weaver to be difficult. (Baltimore Orioles)

to be involved, he didn't want to have to be nice to you because he knew some day he was going to have to tell you that you're out of here, that the Orioles are going to release you. So I just took it one day at a time and tried not to give him any excuse to get rid of me. I tried to avoid him. But he also wanted me to take charge of the pitching staff, which meant we talked every day. It was a constant battle with him.

Jim Palmer saw I could stop the running game. That was the only part of pitching with which Jim thought he had any problem. Jim was in total control of his own game. He told me, "Rick, when I get behind in the count, I want you to set up an inch off the outside corner and call a fastball. That's all you've got to worry about."

Every time when Jim pitched, he would go to Earl and say, "I want Dempsey in there." That way he didn't have to worry about anyone stealing second and scoring on a base hit. That's how my relationship began with Jim.

It wasn't always that easy for me. Earl would bring me in for the pregame meetings, and it seemed like nothing was ever good enough. I made a bad call here, I made a bad call there. But then he always said whatever the pitcher wanted to throw was what he wanted me to call. He also would tell me how he wanted to pitch certain players. One of them was Sixto Lezcano, an outfielder with the Milwaukee Brewers, who batted .285 in 1976 and hit .321 with 28 homers and 101 RBIs in 1979.

Lezcano killed the Orioles. It seemed like all the hits he got off us were on fastballs. So Earl said, "I don't want you to call a fastball to Sixto Lezcano, no matter what." Mike Flanagan was pitching a game for us in Milwaukee, and I called a curveball. Flanny shook me off. Slider, Flanny shook me off. Change-up, same thing. I went through it again. I didn't want to go to the fastball.

Flanny called me out to the mound and said, "I want to throw the fastball. How come you're not calling the fastball?" I told him, "Earl told me not to call a fastball to Sixto Lezcano."

And Flanny said, "Fuck Earl. I'll throw what the fuck I want. Now go back there and call the fastball." I called the fastball, and Lezcano got a base hit. So Flanny was pissed because Earl was right: Sixto could hit anybody's fastball. But they didn't score, so that's all that mattered—except that Earl was pretty angry with me. He said, "Jesus, I told you not to call the fucking fastball. If you don't fucking do what I tell you to do, I'll get somebody fucking else."

That wasn't the first time I heard that from Earl—and not the last. Earl would say those kinds of things, and I would pretend I didn't hear him. He'd literally say, "You're out of the game. I'm putting in the other guy." And I'd put my catcher's equipment on and go back out on the field. He never said anything to me because I think he realized he was over the top a little bit at times.

On April 13, 1979, he made good on the threat to yank me from a game. We were playing on a cold afternoon in Milwaukee, a game we would end up losing 9–3. In the second inning, Larry Harlow was on first base, and I hit a single. Then the pitcher tried to pick Harlow off second and threw the ball into center field. Harlow broke for third, and I broke for second. I got the base easily, and then Harlow for some reason went back to second base. So I scrambled to get back to first but got thrown out, which pretty much killed the inning.

Later in the game, I tried to get around an umpire to catch a foul pop-up and didn't get to it. That was it for Earl. Earl said that "You're out of the ballgame" five or six times, but I put my stuff on anyway and went back out on the field. I was wondering whether or not Earl meant it this time. At the end of the fifth inning, I saw backup catcher Dave Skaggs running in from the bullpen and Earl coming out of the dugout. Earl had to walk a long way to get to the plate. He got there and showed the umpire the lineup card. He said, "Do you see Dempsey's name right there?" He took a pencil and scratched it off on the spot and said, "He's out of the fucking game. And if he doesn't fucking leave, I'm going to forfeit."

I said, "How the hell are you going to forfeit the game, Earl? What the hell are you doing? Go on back to the dugout." I had gotten to the point where I kind of stood up to him because sometimes he just got out of control. But sure as shit, man, Frank Robinson, who was coaching, yelled to me and said, "C'mon Demps, you're out of the game."

When I got off the field, I was so mad at Earl, I took every piece of equipment off and threw it at him from the other end of the dugout. He was standing on the top step in a little Napoleonic stance. My shin guards did kind of a boomerang thing. One shin guard curved away. I threw my chest protector at him, and that didn't go halfway through the dugout. Then I got to my mask and I knew I could hurt him badly if I threw it right at him. So I threw it down at his feet, but it hit a helmet, and the helmet went up and hit him. So he grabbed the helmet and threw it back at me. I caught the helmet and threw it back, and we're going at each other. Everybody's diving out of the way. Finally Frank Robinson grabbed me and said, "Rick, you gotta go. You've got to get off the bench." Robin Yount, my old friend, was laughing his head off on the Milwaukee bench. Each of my teammates was screaming, "Hit him for me!"

So I walked back to the clubhouse so mad that I tore my uniform off. I was down to my jock and my underwear and my socks. And I just walked right into the shower. I'm standing there under the water and all of a sudden I heard the little pitter-patter of feet coming up the stairway and I know it's Earl. So I hid in the back of the shower room. He walked right into the showers and yelled, "Jesus Christ! If I tell you to get out of the fucking game, you've got to get out of the fucking game! I'll get some fat guy in Triple A ball to take your fucking place! You'd better fucking pay attention to me because I'm the boss!"

I turned the hot water off and put the cold water right in the middle of his chest. It was so freaking cold that day. The water hit him in the chest, and he was still screaming at me. He wouldn't budge because he was too proud. He was just getting soaked. Finally, he moved out of that stream of freezing water. He grabbed a towel and walked out, screaming, "I'm the boss!" And I said, "Yeah, Earl, you're the boss. Spelled backward, that's double S-O-B."

The next day I'm back in the lineup again. He never held any of that against me. He just couldn't stand to lose. He would yell and scream at you all the time. That was the way of the world back then with managers screaming and belittling the players just about every day. But that's the way this team responded while he was there. We were good. We didn't go out there on the field to beat the other team. We went out there to beat Earl.

Every time Earl chewed us out and we won, we would try to find a way to get back at him. When he got on the bus after he screamed the whole game about nobody could do this and nobody could do that and you guys suck and you guys are terrible, there were a few guys who would mimic him. John Lowenstein was one of them. "Jesus Christ, somebody hit the outfield grass," Lowenstein would say, capturing Earl's voice perfectly. Earl would look back to see who was saying that, and we all just sat there expressionless. Then Pat Kelly did the same thing. They always could get away with it. I never really did it because I had enough confrontations with him. I didn't want any more. But when he did go overboard with me, everyone knew I would fight back.

Earl won a World Series and guided the Orioles to five 100-win seasons and four American League pennants. He had an incredible .583 winning percentage over 17 years and finished with a losing record only once—in 1986, when he tried in vain to come back and help Baltimore return to glory after a few down years. He was inducted into the Hall of Fame by the veterans' committee in 1996.

Everyone talked about how Earl played for the three-run homer. But no one knew baseball strategy better than Earl. He was the best. Even in this current era, guys are doing things the way Earl did back then. Earl would know exactly how many hits guys got off his pitchers in all situations. He would write it down. They didn't start doing statistical things like that until years after Earl retired. Then everybody kind of got into it, inputting it in computers. Earl did it by memory or writing it down. He would keep notes.

That was the cause of some great battles between Earl and Palmer. They used to argue and fight before the game so much, and Earl would aggravate Jim. I can remember Earl saying, "You know, you can't throw this guy a fastball. He got three hits off your fastball the last time he faced you." Earl knew those kind of stats. Palmer would get mad and upset and say, "You just stay in the dugout and do your own thing and leave me to do the pitching."

It was odd to see a player talk to a manager that way, but that's how everybody had to talk to Earl to gain his respect. There was one time when Earl told Jim not to throw this player a certain pitch, and the guy got a base hit. Earl came out to the mound and said, "I told you not to throw that guy that pitch. You never pay attention to me." Earl's got his hands in his back pockets and he's looking up at Jim. So Palmer looks down and says, "Earl, the only thing you know about pitching is that you couldn't hit it."

When Earl got mad and Jim got mad and walked to the back of the mound, that was my time to get the hell out of there. I didn't want to get in the middle of all those fights. When Palmer was taken out of the game, he would nod. But they had some tremendous battles. And as Jim was walking to the dugout, Earl would rip him the entire time until the reliever showed up.

Earl and I had some tremendous battles, too. There was one time in Toronto, June 19, 1977. It was just a hard game for Earl to handle because we were just getting beat so bad. I remember it got to a point where I was trying to pick guys off the bases because our pitchers weren't going to get anybody out. I threw a ball to third base, it went down the line, and two more runs scored. Earl said, "Get your ass in my office after the game." So the game finally ended, we lost 7–1, and I went to his office. He said, "I want to tell you one thing: you ever throw the ball down the line like that again, I'm going to go get a fat guy out of Triple A ball to take your place!" He was talking about John Stefero, who was working his way up the ladder since 1979 and had finally landed in Rochester. I got so mad. I said, "I'll tell you one thing I'm not going to do, Earl. I'm not going to stop throwing it. It's part of my game. I don't make very many errors, and you shouldn't give a shit about me throwing that one ball. I'm trying to get us out of the freaking inning. You want to get the fat guy out of Triple A ball? Go right the fuck ahead."

He actually took a box that was sitting next to his desk and stood on it so he could be a couple inches taller than me and finger-point me like he did with umpires. I said, "Go ahead, freaking poke me if you want. I don't give a damn what you do." As I walked out the door, four guys fell down on the other side. They were leaning up against the door, listening in. The next day, I was back in the lineup again. That was life with Earl. It was hard, but we won a lot of games.

If you dropped a ball on the field, Earl would rip into you. He cared about the fundamentals. If you messed up one fundamental, you were going to get chastised in front of everybody. And you know what? We were the strongest fundamentally sound team out there and we never dropped balls. It's sort of like the Orioles today under Buck Showalter. We never dropped the ball, even warming up on the sideline. Earl would scream at you across the field if you dropped a ball. That was one of his pet peeves. "Catch the ball" was all he would say.

He went after everybody, and quite a few players on the team went after him. He would just scream and holler so much that he'd push you against the wall where you couldn't take it anymore. Doug DeCinces went after him one time. So did Tippy Martinez, who was my roommate at the time. It was so funny this one time when Tippy came in to pitch and ended up losing the lead. Earl was screaming at him, "You can't walk the first guy when you come in. I'll send your ass back to Triple A ball." Tippy was a mild-mannered guy, but on the plane to Seattle that day, he finally had enough. He had about four or five drinks at that point and said, "I'm an Indian and I don't speak Spanish. Fuck you, Earl." It was his way of telling Earl that he had a different way of dealing with things. I had to calm him down.

Well, Earl had a lot to drink that night, too. Tippy and I got to our room, and there was Earl with a suitcase in his hand, leaning against a door down the hall. Tippy wanted to go after him. I told him to go into the room and unpack and calm down a little bit. So I went up to Earl and said, "Are you where you're supposed to be?" And he slurred back, "I don't know where my room is." I looked at his key and let him in his room. He left his door open, and Tippy ran into the room and shouts, "Don't you ever yell at me again like that. I'm an Indian!" He's drunk, Earl's drunk, and in the end, I had to go in there and get Tippy out of the room.

Tippy finally stepped across that line and stood up to Earl. But that's the way everyone coped with Earl's tirades. You had to confront him. By going after Earl, that's when he realized that he had reached your breaking point.

Not everyone could cope with Earl's gruff personality, though. We had a pitcher, Dave Pagan, who came over in the trade with me from the Yankees. He got chewed out by Earl all the time and he just reached a point where he couldn't take it anymore. So he

During his famous tirades, I think Earl Weaver actually liked it when the umpires argued back. It made it more fun for him. (Baltimore Orioles)

quit baseball and went back to Canada. The guys who learned to stand up to Earl and his yelling, those are the ones who made it.

Some of the most amazing moments were when Earl got into arguments with umpires. There were certain guys who would argue back, which I think made it even more fun for Earl.

I saw him do so many things—such as point a finger at an umpire and stick it inside his mask and poke him on the bridge of the nose. The umpire would turn his back on him, and Earl would run around to the other side. He would kick dirt on home plate. I think that move inspired a lot of minor league managers to try to duplicate what Earl used to do. It was so funny. He would run to second base, pick up the bag, and throw it into center field. A lot of guys have tried to imitate that. But to see it firsthand was the most unbelievable thing I ever saw in baseball.

Earl would stick the bill of his cap inside the umpire's mask and, as he was arguing with him, he would be banging it on the bridge of the ump's nose until it actually got chafed, a little bit scratched, and sometimes even bloody. Sometimes, if Earl really wanted to get into an umpire's face, he would turn his cap backward. That's when he would start poking with his finger.

Earl and Bill Haller—an American League umpire since 1963—went at it more than any two people ever on the field. I think in a way that they both loved each other because Earl had a lot of respect for Haller as being a very good umpire, and Haller, in turn, had respect for Earl as a manager. But once Earl started getting noticed for battling umpires tooth and nail, Haller started to resist a little bit because Earl would get out of control at times. He often took his hat off, threw it on the ground, and unleashed a profanity-laced tirade until he was red in the face.

The most memorable confrontation came one game in September of 1980 when Earl told Haller that he wasn't going anywhere in baseball, that nobody would ever remember him as an umpire, and that in 10 years Earl would be in the Hall of Fame. And Haller threw it right back at him. He said, "What are you going to be in the Hall of Fame for? Blowing the World Series?" Of course, he was referring to 1979, when we lost the last three games to the Pittsburgh Pirates.

But really, it was so much fun at times to watch Earl go on the field and go after an umpire. The things he said to them—the cursing, the swearing—it was just so funny. But he had a passion for it, and that's when the showmanship came out. It escalated because the more the umpire came back at him, the more things Earl would think to do. He used to send messages through me to home-plate umpires about missed strike calls. That's probably why most umpires didn't like me too much, but I was just the freaking messenger!

Earl was quite a showman all the time, as everybody knew, but he was really good at managing a ballgame. Even though I thought Billy Martin was the best manager I had ever seen up to that point, Earl proved to me every day that he was head and shoulders a better manager than all of them. I can remember when he would come to the mound to take out a pitcher he would talk to me about pitching and how he thought I should approach the game. As the relief pitcher was coming in, Earl and I would talk a little bit about baseball. Well, there was a game in Chicago, the bases were loaded, and Earl was coming out to the field. He was annoyed as usual because he was in a situation where he had to change the pitcher. He was talking to me about something and he called for the left-hander, Tippy, to come in. In most cases, of course, a right-hander has a much better chance of retiring a right-handed batter. Same with a southpaw versus a left-handed batter. That's how baseball has worked since the early 1900s. I looked at the hitter, Ron Kittle, a right-handed batter. I said to Earl, "What are doing, bringing Tippy in to face the right-hander? You usually bring him in against lefties." He turned around and looked and went, "Oh my God."

Brooks Robinson came to the mound, and Earl looked at Brooksie and said, "Jesus Christ. Every time I talk to that fucking Dempsey, he confuses me so much. So now I'm bringing in the fucking left-hander to pitch to Ron Kittle." Earl looked at me and said, "Dempsey, don't you ever fucking say anything to me anymore before I make a call out on the mound! I knew who I fucking wanted to bring in, but Dempsey starts fucking talking to me, and I get fucking confused and call for the left-hander instead of the right-hander! When I come out of the fucking dugout, don't you say a fucking word from now on!"

So, Tippy comes in and actually gets Kittle out and gets us out of trouble.

Later that season, we're at home against the Minnesota Twins. We have a situation—runners on second and third with first base open. Dan Ford was hitting, and behind him was Larry Hisle, the RBI leader in the American League. Earl comes out of the dugout and puts up four fingers, which means give Ford an intentional walk to get to Hisle. I want to tell him that Hisle is on deck, but he told me to never, ever talk to him when he's making a decision. I just threw my hands up and said, "Whatever," and started to walk

Ford. I was looking at him every pitch, and Earl was just sitting there. Ball One. Ball Two. Ball Three.

All of a sudden, Pat jumped up on the bench and said, "Skipper! Why are you walking Dan Ford?" Earl answered, "I'm not." And Pat said, "Yes, you are. You're walking Dan Ford to get to Larry Hisle." Earl jumped out of the dugout and said, "No! No! No!" The pitcher is in his windup. It's too late, and he throws the final pitch of the walk. Earl walked back into the dugout with his hands stuffed in his back pockets, shaking his head. So Hisle hit a chopper with the bases loaded, Doug DeCinces couldn't make the play at third, and they scored a run. We got out of the inning, and I got back in the dugout, and Earl was waiting for me. And he yelled, saying, "Why the hell didn't you say something? You know I didn't want to walk Dan Ford." I said, "Earl, you warned me about not to say anything to you when you're on the mound. Whose fucking fault is it now?"

I think Earl had a Napoleonic complex because he was a little 5'7" guy who wanted to prove that he could be the best manager in the game. And he did that. The way he motivated our ballclub was by telling us we couldn't do something. That's exactly the opposite of any manager in the game today. Every manager has got to be pro positive—yes we can, yes we can—trying to build up their confidence. Earl would say, "Jesus, you can't hit this guy today. [Toronto Blue Jays pitcher] Dave Stieb, he strikes us out all the time, gets us out all the time. Can one of you guys make the ball hit the outfield grass, one freaking time?"

Game after game Earl would be screaming in the dugout, "Can't anybody get a hit? This is so pathetic watching this shit, day in and day out." More often than not, we would be trailing and come back to win. And it wasn't about beating Stieb or Toronto, it was about beating Earl because he made life miserable for you if you weren't producing.

After we won, Earl would get so mad because he couldn't say anything on the bus. We were getting him back for all the misery he put us through to make us be productive. I never wanted to say anything to him because the less confrontation I had with him, the better life was.

After Earl retired we lost the fundamentals. Earl was such a pain in the ass with the fundamentals, but he was right. And I think we all realized that. Under Earl, if we took infield practice in spring training and we dropped one ball, we started over again until we could get around the whole infield without making a mistake. He had these idiosyncrasies about him that paid off. It made everybody concentrate on doing things right. For example, when you get the ball, take your time, make a good throw. Make sure the ball goes into your glove. It doesn't matter if you can throw it to the plate without a hop; make sure you hit the cutoff man. That's why we were so good. He beat the fundamental part of the game into us every single day. Five years into my time with the Orioles, Earl was still beating the fundamentals into you on a daily basis.

It's no wonder the Orioles were the best defensive team in baseball at that time. We didn't make mistakes. If you didn't hit the cutoff man, Earl would get on you, and it didn't matter if you were Cal Ripken Jr. or Eddie Murray. Anybody and everybody would hear about it.

I happened to be the guy caught in the middle because there were pitchers he knew he couldn't yell at. He would yell at me when I was standing close to that pitcher so that guy could hear him. That was his way of doing things in the dugout. If Palmer was pitching, he would yell right at him because Jim and Earl fought constantly all the time. If Flanagan was pitching, it was a little bit different. He might say something to Mike the next day, but he would never yell at him at a game. He would say, "Jesus, Dempsey, I told you not to call that pitch! Why the hell do you want to throw him a fastball right there? Why? I told you in the meeting you've got to get this guy out with breaking balls." That's how he would get at Flanagan—by yelling at me.

I thought Earl hated me. My whole career, I thought he hated me because he never said anything positive. Climbing the screen, catching balls near the seats, diving into the grandstand, stepping over the rail, I made some of the greatest catches that you could make from behind the plate. He never said, "Nice play." He always figured the reason you're in the big leagues is because you can make plays like that.

After he died in January 2013, I went to the viewing, and Mary Ann, his wife, told me, "Rick, Earl loved you." I went, "What? You've got to be kidding me, Mary Ann. Every day it was a battle. I just thought the guy couldn't wait to get rid of me. I thought he wanted a left-handed hitting catcher who could hit home runs. He told me that!"

She said, "Rick, that's not what it was all about with him. He would come home and say that he really loved you because he could yell at you all that he wanted and knew you would never quit." When she said that, I couldn't hate the guy anymore. I couldn't hate him anymore because I kind of knew she was right. I understood Earl, I think, better than any manager I ever played for because my father was a really bad alcoholic. He was the greatest guy in the world, but once he started drinking, he wasn't the same person anymore. He would just as soon backhand you as look at you. That's the way he was raised, and that's the way he raised his children: to have respect and to pay attention to everything he said.

I was always hesitant to talk to Earl unless it was about something he wanted me to do in a ballgame. But one day I told myself, I'm going to talk to Earl because I saw him get on the airplane and take five shots—all of them doubles—before the plane even took off. By the time we were five minutes in the air, he was passed out. And he did it day in and day out. I ultimately lost my father the same way. He started drinking at 45 and by the time he was 64 he was dead from it. He ruined his liver.

So one day I pulled Earl off to the side, maybe a year or two before he retired, and said, "Earl, I feel kind of funny saying this, but I kind of worry about you at times." Of course, he snapped back, "Jesus, what the fuck are you talking about? *You're worried about me?* I'm worried about you getting a freaking hit tonight."

I said, "C'mon, Earl. I wish you would stop drinking so much. My father is a lot worse than you are. I wouldn't want to lose my father, although he's very, very tough. I think you're the best manager I've ever seen. And I would hate to see anything happen to you because of your drinking." So he got into this thing, saying, "I'm not an alcoholic. I'm just a heavy drinker. I like it and I think you ought to go out there and worry about getting a base hit and calling a good ballgame. Don't worry about me."

He would piss you off even when you were trying to be nice to him. But you know what? He never forgot that I came to him. Toward the end of his career—after he retired and came back as a manager in the middle of the 1985 season—he brought that story

Earl Weaver speaks to the media in 1986. It wasn't until after his death in 2013 that I found out from his wife how much I meant to him. (Baltimore Orioles)

up. He mentioned to me in a conversation, "You know, you're not so bad. You care about people."

That's when I knew I struck a note with him, telling him what he meant to the game of baseball and how important it was for him to kind of back off from drinking so much. Sooner or later, he would have drank himself to death. And he listened to me. He didn't completely stop drinking, but he limited himself to a couple of drinks a day. So maybe I helped him a little bit.

# Chapter 5

# This Game Is Fun

When I was with the New York Yankees before I got traded in 1976, I was in right field, speaking with relief pitcher Sparky Lyle. Back in those days, even though they fined players for throwing balls into the grandstand, Sparky didn't care. If a section of the fans would yell and scream and holler for him during batting practice, he would throw a ball to whichever group screamed the loudest. I thought that was kind of cool, that he got so many different sections at Yankee Stadium involved in that.

So, he started talking about wanting to go on the tarp during a rain delay and slide on the tarp. I said, "Why would you want to do that? You might get hurt." He said, "I want to do a pantomime of Babe Ruth calling his home run and then I'll run around the tarp and slide, and that will be the end of it." I said, "Well, that might be pretty cool, Sparky."

Then I got traded to the Orioles, and the next year, on the final day of the 1977 season, we were playing the Boston Red Sox for second place. The Yankees had already won the division because the Red Sox eliminated us on Friday, and we knocked them out of it with a win on Saturday. I was in the outfield at Fenway Park on Sunday, throwing baseballs to fans in the stands who were the loudest. It was pretty neat because my teammates kept throwing me balls so I could keep tossing them into the grandstand. They knew that if anyone got in trouble, I was the one who was going to end up paying for the balls. We were having a good time, but then it started to rain. They put the tarp down at the end of batting practice, and by then it was raining pretty heavily. We didn't know if we were going to play the game or not.

Well, there was one baseball left on the tarp, and I said to myself, *I'm going to run out there and grab that baseball and get this whole stadium screaming.* The place was packed because we were still playing for second place. I ran out there, and people started to cheer a little bit just because I ran out on the tarp. The organist started playing "Raindrops Keep Falling on My Head." I picked up the ball and didn't throw it because I wanted everyone there to start singing along with the song. So as I skated around the tarp, everyone started to sing with me. I ran around the bases and I ended up throwing the baseball to the group that sang the loudest. Then I ran off the field, and that was it.

I went into the dugout, and everyone was laughing about it. It was a lot of fun. I went into the clubhouse and was drying off because it was pretty wet out there. All of a sudden, the people in the stadium started pounding on the grandstands with their feet. They were chanting, "We want Dempsey! We want Dempsey!" The clubhouse is right underneath the seating section, so it was deafening when people starting kicking their feet in unison and yelling my name. So Rich Dauer came running in as I was drying off and said, "Demps, they want you to come back out there! Get some baseballs and get back out on the tarp." I said, "No. You know what I'm going to do? The pantomime of Babe Ruth calling his home run. Babe Ruth used to be with the Red Sox. They'll love that!"

I put a pillow in my shirt so I could look a little bit like Babe Ruth. I went out to home plate and pointed to the stands and everyone started to cheer, as if I had already hit the home run. I took two mighty swings, twisting my body as far as it would go. Then I "hit" the long drive to straightaway center field and started to take the home-run trot. Everybody just went crazy. The people were screaming as if I had just hit a home run to win the seventh game of the World Series. I went around the bases and slid into home plate, making a big wave as I sloshed across the tarp. I declared myself safe, the crowd went nuts, and I walked off the field completely drenched.

Yes, that's where it all began. It was a lot of fun because I was flexible enough to get around the field without pulling a muscle or breaking anything. From that point on, every time it got gray or cloudy everywhere we went, one of the team officials would call me up and say, "Can you do your pantomime of Babe Ruth?" One time in Toronto, one of the Blue Jays staffers called me and asked me to do it. I looked up in the stands and saw about 15 people there. I said, "I don't think it's going to work this time."

I did another version of it in Milwaukee one night. But instead of doing a Babe Ruth pantomime, I did one of Robin Yount hitting two home runs in the last game of the 1982 season at Memorial Stadium. I took Robin's jersey. We were childhood friends, and I made him give it to me. I put the pillow in it, which he wasn't too happy about because he didn't want to be fat. After I slid into home plate, Yount came out and took his jersey back. What made that tarp act even more special was that Sammy Stewart came out and pitched to me, as if he was Jim Palmer, who had given up those two home runs. Palmer had been doing commercials for Jockey underwear, so Sammy wore briefs outside of his uniform pants. It wasn't even really premeditated, but Sammy just thought of it at the spur of the moment, went on the field, and did it. Sammy had a way of playing with the ball, flipping it with his hand, that added a nice touch. The people in Milwaukee just loved it.

The only other time I did it was at Memorial Stadium in early July 1978. Same deal—it was a rainy day, and Babe Ruth called his shot. I had to do it at least once at home.

I saw Sparky a year or two after I did it the first time and said, "I finally did what you wanted to do." He told me I did a great job. He still wanted to do it, but by that time, he was too old. Not only that, but the teams and Major League Baseball said they didn't want players running around on the tarp because somebody could get hurt and cost someone a lot of money.

People still come up to me nowadays and talk about it. I think I've met just about every person who was there. They say, "That's the guy who ran around on the tarp." Funny, they don't remember that once in a while I got a hit.

Of course, playing the role of Babe Ruth was only one example of how I had fun with the fans of Baltimore. Orioles fans are unique, and one of the all-time best of them was Wild Bill Hagy.

You have to stay loose because baseball can be a stressful game, and Rich Dauer and I had a pregame routine where we jumped up in the air, did a 360-degree turn, and then slapped our hands together. (Baltimore Orioles)

He was our biggest fan. He drove a cab in the day and showed up at Orioles games at night, always in Section 34. He had a big cowboy hat. He would stand up, start waving his big old cowboy hat to get everyone's attention, and then spell out O-R-I-O-L-E-S with his arms and legs. He was very recognizable and he had his share of beer. But when we really needed a rally, or at least a boost from the crowd, Bill would get the entire stadium to respond to him. It was really the most incredible thing you've ever seen in your life.

Sometimes, Bill would stand on the dugout and do his thing, and I would get up there and join him on the days I wasn't playing. I started spelling out O-R-I-O-L-E-S, too. The fans just bonded with us because we made them so much a part of that energy we had. The relationship we had with those fans was just amazing.

Back in those days, we didn't have guys who got paid to warm up the pitchers in the bullpen during the ballgame. So sometimes it was up to me to do it. A lot of that job consisted of just waiting and watching the game. Some of those times, I'd be sitting on the chair and start thinking, *We really need a rally right here to come back and win this game.* I'd lean back and wave a white flag, trying to get Wild Bill's attention. Well, everyone in Section 34 would start waving back at me. Bill got up to get everybody to start yelling, and I'd do the same thing with the people on my side of the stadium. We had both sides just going wild, and when I started to spell out O-R-I-O-L-E-S from the bullpen, the entire stadium would join in with me. The whole game kind of stopped until we finished.

I'm pretty sure this helped start Oriole Magic in 1979, and it stuck for years and years. It died when the team moved from Memorial Stadium after the 1991 season, and Wild Bill didn't last much longer than that. He went to a few games at Oriole Park at Camden Yards, but it was a different atmosphere. For the fans who watched the Orioles at Memorial Stadium, it was an unforgettable era.

Not all the fun we had in Baltimore occurred on the baseball diamond. We had the Invisible Orioles Magic Band. I lived out in Timonium, Maryland, at that time and in the afternoons I went out to a place called Padonia Station. I would go down there and have lunch before I went to the stadium for the game. One of those times, the band that was playing was called Tiffany. They were practicing their sets before they went on that night. I got to know all the guys in the band, and one time they were practicing the song "Footloose." They couldn't remember all the words, and I knew that song by heart. I stepped up and sang that song. And then I started to sing a few other songs, and they asked me to come in some night and sing with the band. It seemed like every weekend we were home, I would go to the bar after the game and sing a 10-song set. We just had the best time ever! A lot of the guys, including Cal Ripken Jr., heard I was doing this, so they would show up. Sometimes, even some of the players from the other team would stop by. We just packed the place.

After a while I went to a recording studio and did a few songs with the band. And then in 1986, I got some of my teammates to come out before batting practice, and they set up a drum set and a little stage, and we would lip-synch songs that I had already recorded. Eddie Murray was the drummer, I was the vocalist, Mike Boddicker was on one of the guitars, Rich Bordi was on another guitar, and Ralph Salvon was on the keyboard. Floyd Rayford, Ken Dixon, and John Habyan had parts in it, too. They took some film of it and sold the video at the stadium. Naturally, we didn't get a cut.

I was Cal's roommate for his first three years in the big leagues, and he was a pretty good prankster. We had good clean fun. Nothing crazy like swallowing goldfish or eating glass. I could pretty much pick any lock of any hotel we stayed in or find some way to get a key to get in somebody's room. Tom Marr, who died in July 2016, was our play-by-play guy, and we just had the best time with him because he never got too upset with what we did to him and, let me tell you, we terrorized this poor guy. We took fire extinguishers, stuck the nozzle under his door, and filled the room with foam. It eliminated oxygen, so pretty soon it would force him out of the room. After the room would air out a little bit, he would go back inside, but it was funny when we checked on him in the morning because when he got out of the bed it looked like he was making a snow angel. There was a perfect impression of his whole body.

We'd see him in the bar talking with Earl Weaver and some of the coaches, getting his information for the next game, and Cal and I would sneak into his room and start getting down to business. First, we'd put a bucket of water over the bathroom door so he would get drenched when he walked in. Then we'd put cellophane over the toilet and then hide in the shower to see the results. After he got soaked by the bucket, he'd try and take a leak, and piss would splash all over his legs and pants. He didn't even look down until he was completely covered in piss. After that, he'd dry off and go to bed—except we'd put pine needles in the sheets, so when he rolled over they'd stick through and get him. Oh, and we'd also put his pillow in water so it splashed when he lay down. We even glued his toothbrush and hairbrush to the bathroom counter so he couldn't pick them up.

I miss Tom, who was 73 when he died. He had a stroke after undergoing back surgery and never recovered. He was never going

Cal Ripken Jr. was a huge prankster. He and I used to terrorize our buddy, play-by-play guy Tom Marr. (Baltimore Orioles)

to be able to speak again, so it would have been an awfully frustrating life. He was huge part of the Orioles' success. We had so much fun with him, and he brought our games to life on television. He worked with Chuck Thompson, and what a great team that was.

During one spring training in the 1980s, Tippy Martinez, Lenny Sakata, Boddicker, and I were all living together. They might have been the three cheapest guys on the planet. Every time we went someplace—breakfast, lunch, or dinner—I'd always get stuck with the bill. So we were at this dinner place across from the Grapetree Apartments, where we were living in Key Biscayne. We had a nice dinner, the four of us, and then at the end of dinner, I ended up getting stuck with the bill again. I never complained about it, really, but this time it kind of annoyed me because I knew I was getting worked. They were doing it on purpose.

Anyway, as I was going back to the table to leave a tip, I noticed that one of the guys left his room key on the table. I put it in my pocket, and as we were driving back, which took just two or three minutes, I was thinking that when they went underneath the building to park the car that I would run into their apartment and hide in the closet and get my revenge.

That spring there was a guy in Key Biscayne who was robbing a lot of people late at night at gas stations or convenience stores—just about everywhere and anywhere. We were warned to be careful of this guy, whom they called *El Guapo*. I raced into the apartment closet, which had the kind of slats in it where you could see at an angle. So I was in there and I heard Tippy call his wife on the phone. He was lying in the bedroom. Lenny went into the bathroom, and Boddicker went into the other back room. I couldn't tell what he was doing. So I came out of the closet and went into the kitchen. I had the same unit in my building, so I knew where everything was. And I turned all the power off in the apartment and ran back into the closet.

I heard Tippy talking to his wife and he was saying, "Oh, honey, all the lights went out! Don't hang up because you know I'm afraid of the dark." I was pinching myself because I was giggling. Lenny, meanwhile, was sitting on the toilet and he yelled, "Hey, somebody turn the lights on so I can find some toilet paper in here!" Boddicker came out of his room, went in the kitchen, and finally turned the power back on after about seven or eight minutes.

I was listening to them bitch and complain, and then finally they all got together in the kitchen. They were playing poker with nickels, dimes, and quarters—of course, they wouldn't play for any real cash. I saw their reflection from the mirror in the dining room. So I opened the door and threw a hairbrush over the middle of the card table. One of them yelled, "Son of a bitch," and another said, "Who the hell is that?"

I responded: "Hey gringos, this is El Guapo. I no want to be identified. I want you take the money out of your pockets and put it on the table. I don't want no problem. Okay? What your name?" So Tippy said, "Tippy Martinez." And I said, "Oh, you're no gringo. You speak Spanish?" He said, "No." I asked, "So why not? Listen, you guys, you no go for door and try to get away. Do what I tell you. Leave the money, and there will be no problem."

Lenny went down on his knees to pray, and I said, "I see you, little pig. You say mini-prayer, fine, put your money on the table." Tippy goes to the kitchen and opens up the drawer and pulls out four butter knives and a can opener. As a result, I said, "You, Martinez, what you got?"

"I've got knives," he said.

"What, you think I stupid? You have a knife, but I have a gun."

I held them at bay for around 30 minutes. Then Sakata moved toward the panic button near the door, and I said, "Hey, Gringo, you take another step, and I'm going to cap your ass. You want to be the first one to die?"

Boddicker whispered to them, "Let's make a run for it," and, of course, I said, "Hey, you try to make a run for it, and I'll shoot all of you and take your money anyway. Now, leave the money on the table and go in the back room." And they did.

So I got their money, went out the sliding glass door, and ran away. I got back to the room, and Cal and I watched outside as a horde of policemen came up in their cars, and it was a crazy scene. The newspaper article said: four Baltimore Orioles were robbed at their apartment last night, and the burglar got away with $4,000. It wasn't more than about $27 total. They thought they were going to get some extra money from the insurance company.

So I took all the money and put it in front of their lockers, and man, were they mad. Of course, they knew why I did it—because they never paid for a damn meal. Those guys were so damn cheap, I still think Tippy has his meal money buried in a pot somewhere.

One reason why I liked to keep things light is there was a lot of pressure on the players back then. Guys didn't make as much money as they do now, so they needed playoff money and they needed World Series money. Everybody took it a lot more seriously than they do today because many of the players in the game now are already making millions of dollars. Back when I played, many of the players had to work in the winter to pay the bills. The pension program wasn't what it is now either, so the game became very stressful. So to keep guys loose, to keep them in the right frame of mind to go play baseball, you needed a few antics once in a while. I wasn't the only guy. Dauer was a character, as was Todd Cruz. If there was a prank to pull, those guys tried to get involved. Cal was definitely a prankster, too.

One of the classic pranks was the hot foot. When I wasn't playing, I needed something to do, and often the hot foot was my way of keeping busy. At Memorial Stadium you could look around the corner from down in the runway, put your hand up there, and put the match in the guy's shoe. Boddicker and Benny Ayala—or anyone else who seemed too wrapped up in the game to pay attention to us—were often the targets. After I stuck the match in the side of their shoe, I had to find a way to light it without drawing attention. If Earl and the other coaches saw you, you'd get in a ton of trouble. But the payoff was worth it. If a guy was sitting back in the bench and didn't see the light flare up, it was so damn funny. Our trainer, Ralph Salvon, once had a pair of shoes that he got from a department store, and they were anything but top quality. They were more plastic than anything else. He wore them with his trainer's outfit. Ralph was sitting there one night and, of course, he couldn't see over his belly because it was so big. I remember lighting the matches, and the flame flared up massively. I was actually thinking, *Oh my God, we're going to put him in the hospital!* When it heated up and started to melt the side of his plastic shoe, you've never seen a guy that big move so fast. He was a 280-pound bowling ball, and it was incredibly funny to see him jump up and start running through the dugout, taking out players like they were duckpins. I'm glad he didn't get hurt because it lit him up pretty good.

Ralph was one of our frequent victims. He'd be sitting on the edge of the training table, and we'd pull him down and tape him to the table. He didn't have enough strength to break the tape because we'd use about 20 rolls of it. Palmer was part of that, too. (Don't let him tell you he wasn't.) We taped Ralph's knees, his waist, his stomach and tied both his hands under the table. He was there to stay. Unless you cut him loose, he was going to stay there until the end of time. We put a mouthpiece over him so nobody would hear him and then we'd walk out on the field for the start of the game. Eventually, Earl would go, "Where the fuck is Ralph? He should be sitting out here on the bench." So then we'd have to go cut him loose, maybe around the third inning. Ralph was totally pissed, but after five minutes, he'd get over it.

Our ballclub was really close during the 1980s, and I really enjoyed all the fun and great things we used to do. There was a golf course down in Florida where they filmed the movie *Caddyshack*. It was called the Rolling Hills Golf Club and now it's the Grande Oaks Golf Club. We played there all the time. We were so competitive, even though none of us were really good golfers because we had just picked up the game. I might have been a 15-handicap, Tippy-was a 20, Lenny was a 3—he was the only one who was really good—and Tim Stoddard was about a 15 or 20.

We went out to the course one day and, because we were so competitive, everybody cheated. If you found your ball before the other guys found you, you'd drop another ball or kick it out of the weeds and go, "Oh, here it is!" Tippy was notorious for that. We were playing best-ball, two-man teams, and on this one particular hole, Lenny was on in regulation, and I had to make a good shot. My ball rolled down the hill and was half underwater right on the bank. Because I was right-handed, I had to stand in the water. But the water would have been up to my knees because it got deep quickly. I was determined I wasn't going to give a stroke away and drop the ball because Lenny would have won the hole.

So I took my pants off. We're right near the highway, and I was standing there in my tidy whities. Everybody was laughing because I was setting up to take a shot in a white shirt and white underwear with no shoes. I took a practice swing with one eye on the ball and the other looking out for fucking alligators. I didn't give a shit because I'd have fought an alligator to make a chip shot that would get me near the flag for a par. So I walked in the water, and, of course, the guys were shouting, "Gator! Gator!" I'm obviously nervous, and all the cars that drive by were honking because they saw me in my underwear. They weren't boxer shorts, but they were pretty short. Not quite Palmerish—he wore a damn thong—but white and short nonetheless. I finally took the swing and hit a pretty good shot. I ran out of the water as soon as the ball took off to avoid getting snapped at by a freaking alligator. I don't remember if I hit the putt, but I do remember Stoddard doubled over on the fairway, laughing his ass off.

Baseball players going at it in golf usually features something crazy happening, especially when there's pride and cheating involved. As soon as our morning spring training practice was over, we'd head to the golf course in Key Biscayne. One time Tim had something bad to eat for lunch and was beginning to feel it on the green. He said, "Man, I've got to go to the bathroom really bad," but we said, "You've got to take this shot." We were rushing him, saying, "C'mon Tim, we've got people waiting on the fairway behind us."

So he took the club back and swings and shits his pants. *Holy fuck! He got it all over his white shorts.* We were literally doubled over with laughter. Tim Stoddard was fucking 6'7" and he's got diarrhea coming down his legs. Tippy wouldn't even get near the cart because Tim was sitting in it. We didn't wear golf socks back in those days. We had the sanitary socks we took from the club-house. Tim yelled, "Tippy! Tippy! Help me! Give me your sani-taries!" So Tippy took his socks off and gave them to Tim, who headed in the mangrove to go clean himself off. There are bugs and crabs back there, but Tim didn't care. He was tripping along, trying to take his pants off and wipe his ass. We were on the fair-way, busting apart watching him.

We saw two ladies coming up in a golf cart and we kind of snuck away from the scene. They look into the mangroves and see Tim bent over, butt naked, trying to wipe all the shit off his legs. One lady said, "Oh, my God! We shouldn't be here." They bolted out of there.

Tim got himself cleaned up, even though you could still smell him a half a hole away. We got to a par 3, and Tippy hit his ball in the water. I knew it was in the water because I saw it fucking splash. Tippy said, "I'll look for it anyway." I chipped up with a pretty good shot, and Tippy was still looking for his ball. Finally I heard, "I got it." So he hit the ball up, really close to hole. I go up to mark the shot, and there was this old fucking golf ball that's been lying in the sun for about three fucking months. It's got a gash in the side of it, and now I know why it sort of flopped as it rolled—because it wasn't really a round golf ball. I said, "Tippy, you got to be shitting me. You're telling me that's your ball?" And he said, "Yeah, I bladed it as I hit it. I must have put a cut on the side of it." I said, "You lying fuck! What a cheater."

Finally, we got to the 18th hole. Stoddard and I still had a chance to beat Tippy and Lenny, who could really drive the ball at that time. They had a little cabana on the right where people could stop and get a drink or a snack. Lenny hit the ball and shanked it real bad. Everyone at the cabana was watching him from the patio, and all of a sudden, they're diving out of the way because the ball was headed right toward the middle of the bar. The ball hit down and bounced into the bar, scattering the bartender and everyone in the place. The ball was on one of the slats, the kind they have at bars so you don't have to walk on the slimy floor. Lenny looked out the back door and noticed he had a pretty good view of the green. So he wanted to hit the ball. I said, "Bullshit, it's out of bounds!" But no, Lenny said, "I don't see any white tape so I can hit it out of there." There was a guy at bar who was shit-faced drunk. He was the only one who didn't move, even though the ball only missed him by six inches. So Lenny said, "I wonder what club I should use to hit off these slats." And the guy said, "I tell ya what. You should use a club soda, that's what the fuck you should use."

After we won the World Series in 1983, camera crews started to follow us around at spring training. They wanted to see what we did after practice to have a good time together. We were playing golf one day, and I was using orange balls. We were just stupid rookies at golf, using balls that were colored Oriole orange. Anyway, I hit a pretty good shot up on the green. While everybody else was getting ready to hit, a damn raccoon ran up and took my ball. I started running after the raccoon, and the cameraman caught me going into the palmetto bushes in pursuit of the animal and my ball. After about 10 seconds, I found the damn raccoon. He reared up me and started hissing at me, and that's when

I realized I no longer gave a shit about getting my ball. I ran out of there, looking like a tribe of Indians was chasing me. "The fucking thing is rabid," I yelled. "Everybody run!"

I had some friends down in Florida who would give me their boat to use, a nice little 20-footer. We'd throw our clubs in the back and shoot over to the Miami Country Club. You had to tee off at a certain time because if it got too dark you couldn't see the sandbars coming back. That was news to me. I wasn't that knowledgeable about the water around Key Biscayne. It all looked pretty deep to me. Well, we were heading back, and I could see the light of the marina. I made a beeline for it. I had this boat going full blast, trying to get back before the water got too shallow. Everyone was clutching the side, certain I was going to hit something, but we made it back okay.

The five of us were going to go fishing the next day. That's the time of year when the blacktip sharks are mating. There are thousands of them out there, and we were going to catch ourselves a few. So we went out in broad daylight, around 2:00 PM, and I hit three sandbars a mile off shore. We got stuck on the last one. I said, "Two of you guys are going to have get off the board and push it, so I can get enough traction to get off this sandbar." Gary Roenicke jumped off the back of the boat and told us, "You guys better be watching out for those damn sharks, man."

He was probably up to his waist, and you could see the sharks swirling in the shallow water. We're nervous as hell, but Roenicke was out there, rocking the boat. I revved it pretty good, and it was kicking up a lot of sand, which got the attention of the sharks. They're closing in, and Roenicke gave it a good shove. I jolted forward about 15 feet, leaving Rhino covered with mud and standing there waist deep, and here came the sharks. He screamed, "You cocksuckers! Get back here!" It was about a minute before I got him out of there.

Sammy brought his family to spring training. His son, Colin, went out fishing with us one day. The camera crew was filming us, and poor Colin couldn't catch a thing. He was trying hard but just too young to get the hang of it. In his southern drawl, Colin said, "Ah jest can't catch a fish. They won't bite my hook." I said, "Don't worry about it, kid, I'm going to dive in the water and catch a fish." I threw my fishing pole down and jumped in the water. What he didn't see is that I took one of the fish we already caught. I stuck it in my pants, then pulled it out, and bit it in the lip so it started wiggling. I put it in my mouth and came up from the water. Colin's eyes got so big! "Mr. Dempsey, he caught a fish in his mouth?" he yelled. Colin was around five or six at the time. The poor kid died of cystic fibrosis when he was 11.

When Freddy Lynn was with our ballclub, we were doing pretty well fishing one day and had caught about 10 or 15 fish when it started to rain. They had one of those little houses out on the water where you could pull up your boat and get some lunch. It was raining hard enough where you had to get under cover, so I brought the boat into one of those little places. All of a sudden, the clouds drop a downpour on us. We're underneath a platform with wood slats, and it turned out that the birds love to shit on those platforms. As soon as that rainstorm hit, all of that duck shit started pouring down on Lynn. The boat was covered with shit, and so was everyone in the boat. Mostly Freddy, who was coated with seagull shit, pelican shit, and duck shit.

The Yankees enjoyed a good prank, too. When I was in New York, Fritz Peterson and Mike Kekich were the ones who swapped families. One day we all went out to Sawgrass. They were having some water issues out there; the levels were low. It made the fishing a lot better because the fish congregated together a little bit more. Catfish Hunter, Fritz, Kekich, Thurman Munson, and I rented a boat. I was walking out to the boat, and the mud got so soft that I slipped down into the muck up to my knees and I couldn't move. I was holding on to the aluminum boat so I wouldn't sink any deeper. Well, at that point, Kekich saw this little alligator that was about two or three feet long. He saw it on a bank and he chased it away. It froze right there about four or five feet from me. It was enough to be afraid of. Fritz got an oar out and started to slap at the little alligator to move it up more on the land, so he could catch it. But instead of running away, it moved like a curveball and started heading back for me. I had nowhere to go because I was stuck. I had one leg in the boat and the other knee deep in the mud. The alligator came right at me. It went right under me as my whole life flashed in front of me. I would have gotten castrated if that alligator had just looked up about two inches. That one got away, but Fritz ended up corralling another one. All the alligators were up on the shore because the water wasn't deep enough.

Fritz took one of those alligators to the ballpark and put it in the whirlpool. They didn't turn the hot water on, but they put the cold water in there. Gene Michael was going to get into the tub before practice that day. Gene stuck his toe in and then suddenly saw the alligator in there. He jumped higher than he did when the mouse was in his jock! Everybody was waiting for it to happen, and, let me tell you, you've never seen anyone run out of a room faster than he did.

# Chapter 6

## From Behind the Plate

Although I learned a lot in the Minnesota Twins organization and with the New York Yankees before I got to Baltimore, I got my opportunity to play every day with the Orioles. And one of the guys who had the biggest impact on me was Jim Palmer.

Jim made it simple and he made me understand what pitching—and what you want a starting pitcher to do on the mound—was all about. The first day I got a chance to catch Jim in a ballgame, he pulled me aside and said, "Rick, if I ever get behind in the count, just remember this one thing: sit an inch off the outside corner and call for the fastball." He truly did command that side of the plate, down and away. He made me believe that's the most important pitch in all of baseball. If a pitcher can throw an inch off the corner every single time he's behind in the count, he should win 20 games; there's no doubt about it. And Palmer won 20 or more games in eight different seasons and went 15–5 when he was 36 years old. He finished 268–152, won the Cy Young Award three times, and, of course, was an overwhelming choice to enter the Hall of Fame in 1990.

Palmer had an insight to the game that I really did appreciate. I thoroughly enjoyed listening to him talk about pitching and hitters. One thing I was known for most was asking questions. When I came to the big leagues weighing less than most bat boys, no one gave me much of a chance of making it. So I figured I needed to learn as much as possible to have a chance to stay in the big leagues for a long time. Knowing that Palmer was the best pitcher in baseball at that time, I wanted to find out everything I could from him. He was a power pitcher. There were finesse guys on the team, and there was a definite difference between them and Jim.

Jim Palmer had a huge impact in improving my performance because he was such an insightful player. (Baltimore Orioles)

The way Palmer pitched up in the strike zone is probably something he couldn't do in today's game. The way the ball travels, the way it's wound up a lot tighter than it used to be, coaxing a batter to hit a fly ball now is a dangerous thing because even the little guys can go 10, 15 rows deep without hitting it very hard. But in Palmer's day, he could get a lot of outs and make the pitch count stay low by throwing high fastballs. He got a lot of strikeouts, but there were guys he knew he could retire without using five or six pitches.

When I sat with Jim before the game to talk about how he wanted to orchestrate his outing, he would say, "I'm going to throw this guy a high fastball and get him out of there in one or two pitches." He knew exactly how many pitches it would take to get a guy out. His memory of all the hitters through the league, and guys who had gotten key base hits off him, was unmatchable. His recall was incredible, as you can even see today in his work as a color analyst. He was amazing.

I remember a guy we always had a tough time getting out was Bruce Bochte, who started his career with the California Angels and also played for the Cleveland Indians, Seattle Mariners, and Oakland A's. He was a left-handed hitter who had a lot of motion with his batting stance. He would always seem to get big hits against us that would hurt the ballclub. So I asked him: "How do you get Bochte out, Jim?" And he said, "The pitch he has trouble with because of all that movement is a hard slider, down and in. You'll get under the swing." And so I tried it. Boddicker could throw the slider down and in, so could Steve Stone. When we started to throw Bochte that one particular pitch, we really started to limit the hits he got against us.

I used to pick Jim's brain about little things like that. Jim Spencer of the Yankees got a lot of key hits off Palmer's fastball. He could handle that. He didn't swing at the high fastball; he made Jim bring it down and away. Palmer started getting him out by throwing a change-up, which was his third best pitch. It didn't make Jim feel comfortable that he had to go to his third best pitch to get somebody out, but the bottom line was that he finally figured out a way to get Spencer outta there. We keyed each at-bat against him to set him up for that straight change. He would throw the fastball up and in, see if we could maybe get a foul ball and get into a situation where we could get him out in front of the pitch. It wouldn't necessarily be a strikeout, but maybe a ground ball double play.

Jim was truly fantastic on the mound—very arrogant and very knowledgeable. What people don't understand about Jim is that he always wanted to help everyone, even the opposition. He would talk to them after he retired. He would say, "This is how you get this guy out. This is how you get that guy out." What he doesn't realize is that he's telling guys how to beat the Orioles. But he really owns such a wealth of knowledge and he felt compelled to share it.

Jim had so many things going for him during his playing days beyond his incomparable skill on the diamond. He was a good-looking guy. He did a slew of commercials, most notably for Jockey underwear. He was articulate, he was smart, and he knew how to pitch better than anybody I've ever been around.

In 1991, at the age of 45 and seven years after he retired, Jim attempted to make a comeback with the Orioles. I knew that Jim, just using his brain, could win a ballgame. But he benefited from the connection of being both smart and fit. He was physically capable of doing almost anything when he was in his prime. I could line up on the outside corner and close my eyes, and he wouldn't just hit the glove; he'd put it in the pocket. That's how good he really was. He was incredible. But time catches up with all of us and it finally got to Jim. He finally hung it up in the middle of May in 1984 at age 38 after going 0–3 with a 9.17 ERA. His comeback failed when he got injured in spring training, but by that time, the guy had already done it all.

Truth is, as Palmer reached the back end of his career, he wasn't as perfect as when he was young. Early on, when they'd come to take him out of ballgames, he wasn't looking over his shoulder for the bullpen to come to save him. No way. He'd tell Earl Weaver, "Who are you thinking about bringing in?" And after the manager said, "I'm going to bring in this guy," Jim would say: "Oh, no, you're not. I'm going to finish the game." And Weaver would take it because Jim just wasn't coming off the mound. Jim had a relationship with Earl, in which he would tell him what he was going to do, and Earl was willing to accept it because let's face it: there wasn't a better pitcher on the staff. Jim wanted to go nine innings and he usually did. Look at the record book. He pitched 211 complete games over his career. He got paid for wins and he didn't want to jeopardize that by having some reliever come in and blow a game. He wanted to be totally responsible for his own game.

But as time went on, you could tell that Jim realized he couldn't do some things anymore. And he basically wanted someone to help him at that point. He wanted someone to come out of the bullpen and take up those last two innings. At that point in his career, there were things that started to affect him like the heat or just plain fatigue. He had 24 complete games over his last six seasons—none in the last two—after having 19 in 1978 alone. It's just that he didn't feel as good late in ballgames as he did when he was younger, and he would basically ask out of a few games. It was like, "I've had it, I'm done, you can bring in someone who probably has better stuff than me right now." He was tremendously smart about it, but it wasn't the same Jim Palmer who I started to catch in 1976 when I first got traded over here.

Jim was amazing when it came to reading hitters, and I learned from him. Another thing Jim was really good at was evaluating the pitchers on the Orioles, like Flanagan and Boddicker, and how we should orchestrate our games. Steve Stone was a finesse guy all the way. He pitched off his curveball. His curveball was the best in the game one year after he came to us in 1979. He was about a .500 pitcher until he came to the Orioles. With our defense and the hitters that we had, it was easy for him to really fit into our system and flourish. He went 11–7 that first year and then 25–7 in 1980, when he won the Cy Young Award.

But with Palmer, whenever I had a question, I would go ask him. I'd ask him what pitch to go to when the game was on the line, what pitches to throw to certain guys, when to pitch a guy in, how to read batters. Before I met Jim, I learned how to read batters by talking with guys like Bob Rodgers, who was a catcher with the Twins, and Jim Hegan, who was a retired catcher who worked with the Yankees when I was there.

You learned who the pull hitters were, how to pitch to them, and how to pitch to a spray hitter. Every team has someone in the order that can hit to all fields, hits for a high average, can drive in runs, and hit any pitch. You had to learn how to handle him. And on the other side, you had to identify the finesse pitchers on your team and the power pitchers. You had to figure out how a power pitcher is going to get out a spray hitter or someone who hits it on the ground and uses his speed to get on base.

Jim and I often talked about how to get out great hitters who went to the opposite field, like Rod Carew. Palmer was not only knowledgeable about the throwing mechanics, but also the philosophy of the game. He was tremendous at evaluating hitters and pitchers and game situations. He knew when to challenge a guy—try to blow it past him—or when to throw the ball over the plate, let him hit it, and let the defense do its thing.

It all started to open up to me when I got here to Baltimore and got to talk to some of the better pitchers in baseball. Sometimes I would even sneak some questions in to guys who weren't even on my team. I talked to Mel Stottlemyre and Catfish Hunter when I was with the Yankees and maintained that bond after I left. Catfish was a fascinating guy. He didn't have overpowering stuff, but he had an incredible command of the strike zone. He used to throw sliders up and in, which is unheard of. He threw a cut fastball under the hands of the big powerful right-handed hitters. They'd see the ball up and figure this was a chance to hit the ball out of the park. But at the last second it had a two-inch movement, and that's where Catfish would get so many outs. He would bait them up to swing at a pitch, and all of a sudden, it wasn't there. You could see how much that pitch did for Mariano Rivera. It was the same cut fastball that Catfish had. Mariano made a Hall of Fame career out of it.

These are the kind of things I learned along the way. As time goes by, if you can stay healthy yourself and stick around, that kind of information is invaluable. You try to give it to today's catchers, though they don't really care to listen. You want to talk about game philosophy and how you can help get them into the seventh inning with your starter, but they don't want to hear it.

Palmer realized that baseball was an endurance sport, and the way to get deep in ballgames was to have strong legs and a strong heart. You had to be durable, so Jim was on a running program. I could appreciate that because I was on the track team in high school. I ran the half mile in 2:05 and the mile in 4:26. I ran a lot and, even though I loved it, I didn't realize how much of an affect it would have on me in my professional career. I could catch three games a day because you couldn't wear me out. I wasn't a big guy. It took me six years in the big leagues to go from 162 pounds to 180, the weight at which I played for most of my career. But I had that endurance; I could back up first base on every ground ball, and it never wore me out. Palmer was the same way. After Jim was done with his spring training start, he would go in the outfield and run line to line at a very fast pace 20 times. I would go out there with him and push the pace. The ego got to him because he thought he was the only one who could run that much, that fast. But the main reason I was out there was to build camaraderie with him. I knew I'd need that down the road.

Everything Palmer did, he thought he had to do it perfectly. There was another guy like that—Cal Ripken Jr. Jim had to excel at everything he did. He took up golf and became a scratch golfer. He's a 2 or 3-handicap right now. He took up tennis, and when they told him it would have an impact on his pitching arm, he learned to play left-handed. Jim just didn't want to get beat at anything. So you loved being his teammate because that's what we were there for. We were all good friends, but we were there to win. He knew he couldn't pitch every day, so when he wasn't on the mound, he would tell other people what they had to do to win.

Everybody on the Orioles tolerated Jim telling them what to do because this team was always about winning. Some people who were never going to be as good as Jim and didn't have the work ethic that Jim had probably took his advice the wrong way. Those guys should have listened. Jim was a positive influence on Dave McNally, Mike Cuellar, Pat Dobson, almost everyone. That's the way they did it back in those days. Palmer made it look easy and was glad to share the knowledge.

We always had fun with Jim because he did those underwear commercials. The women loved him. He was the best-looking athlete in the game at that time, and when he did those commercials, not much was left for the imagination. I did a commercial with him one time but told him I would not put on the underwear. I did the commercial bare from the waist up.

Funny thing is, Jim was very modest. He wore a bathrobe on the set, but when he took the robe off and they started filming, his entire package was there for the world to see, and he was very embarrassed. And then as soon as his line was done, he ran to put that robe back on. But yeah, the women—beautiful women—loved him. In my fan club, there wasn't one woman under 200 pounds. Good for him, though, I get it.

Back in 1982, when we lost down the stretch to the Milwaukee Brewers, Jim had been 13–1 since May 30. He ended up pitching that last game against the Brewers for a playoff berth. Well, Robin Yount hit two home runs off him that day, and the Brewers won the game 10–2. It wasn't like Jim to lose a big game. Imagine going essentially the whole summer without losing a game and then losing the biggest game of the year. But I guess time caught up to him, and the odds caught up to him. He pitched in only 19 games over the next two years before hanging it up.

When he made his ill-fated comeback, he obviously wasn't the same guy. He realized pretty quickly that it wasn't worth ruining the memory of a brilliant career by pitching at 50 percent of what he was before. Why did he come back? Well, he had a little break, then got into the Hall of Fame, and maybe thought he could make it as a 45-year-old on his brain alone. But I don't think he realized it was going to take a whole lot more than that. The game was changing. Some pretty good players were coming into it with a lot of strength and power in their bats.

It hurt Jim to lose ballgames. As his career wound down, he just realized he wasn't going to have that good fastball that he always had, he wasn't going to be able to spot it where he always did. Not only that, but the curveball didn't snap the way it used to. He got through games using his brain, but that only goes so far. You've got to have good, physical ability to pitch on a regular basis.

I think the game had changed, and Jim Palmer is the reason, to a degree, why teams now use a five-man rotation. Toward the end of his career, the Orioles realized that pitching in a four-man rotation took too much out of Jim. So they decided to put him in a five-man rotation. It was Palmer who forced every organization to take a better look at their more talented pitchers and realize that putting them in a five-man rotation was going to help make their careers last longer. Now you see today there's no way that anyone would ever go back to a four-man rotation.

We used to tease Jim Palmer about the Jockey underwear ads he did. Despite his good looks, he is actually a modest guy. (Baltimore Orioles)

\* \* \*

The first time I saw Mike Flanagan, I was on the New York Yankees, and he had just been called up by the Orioles. And yeah, I was his first major league strikeout. He never let me forget that! I was also Rollie Fingers' last strikeout and I saw both of them at some event much later, and both of them had fun ribbing me about that. But hey, there were a lot of guys who struck me out, so they shouldn't have felt too good about it.

I found out quickly that Mike was a quiet guy, liked to stay to himself. I think Palmer made a point of bringing Flanny's personality out, at least to a degree. Through the years of working together, those guys were incredible. Mike had a dry sense of humor but really had a way of putting us in stitches when he wanted to. When he said something, everybody listened.

On the diamond Mike was as tough a pitcher as I have ever caught and ever seen in this game. Pitch count meant nothing to him. He could have been a power pitcher, he could have been a finesse pitcher. He had a two-seam fastball that sometimes would break away from the left-handed hitters. That was the pitch that tore a ligament and a piece of bone off my knuckle. I stayed in games and caught, but whenever I would catch a pitch in the pocket of the glove, I had to wait 30 seconds to a minute to get feeling back in my hand. Finally, I had a doctor inject it, and it dissolved the bone. Finally that sensation went away.

Flanagan threw a heavy, heavy fastball. He had two or three different kinds of breaking balls. He had a curveball, a side-armed curveball, a cut fastball, and a change-up. He worked on everything. He would throw you the kitchen sink out there because he had these different deliveries and different pitches. He was the strongest guy I ever caught. In Game 1 of the 1979 World Series, he threw 154 pitches. Do you think there's a pitcher in the game today who would even consider doing that? And we won the game 5–4. Mike was mentally tough. You just couldn't get him out of ballgames, just like Palmer. He adopted that philosophy that you're just not going to get me out of this game. He was going to do it all himself.

He won the Cy Young Award in 1979, going 23–9 with five shutouts and 16 complete games. He just got on a roll. Mike had a fastball he could spot inside and away, and the movement on his two-seam fastball was incredible. It moved in, it moved out. And we developed a sidearmed curveball that we used maybe once or twice a ballgame. It was always in a situation when we needed a big out, maybe a double play or a strikeout. When he stepped almost right at the left-hand hitter and flipped that sidearm curveball to the outside corner, most guys just couldn't hit it.

Mike was strong, and it was partly because he worked with Palmer. They ran from line to line, back and forth, on the field. You don't really see guys do that anymore. They jog now to center field, and that's it. Palmer and Flanagan ran 20 hard sprints from line to line. That's like running a 220-yard sprint. They pushed each other, running hard in the summer heat. It set a precedent for everyone on the team. The starters would run 20 of them, and the relievers did 16. We were in shape. It's the reason why: if we were within five games of you at the All-Star break, we were going to win the pennant.

The only thing Mike had an issue with was pitching with men on base. He wasn't the best at throwing over to first or keeping guys close. They got some good jumps on him a few times. So Earl Weaver wanted him to come out when he was pitching between starts to work on keeping the runner close to the base. Mike didn't think it was all that important, and looking back, maybe Mike was right. But Earl was adamant about it, so Mike worked on it between starts. I was warming him up on the side of the field at Memorial Stadium, and Mike went to the set position. All of a sudden, Earl started running down the left-field line. Everyone was looking at him, wondering what the heck was going on. Well, Earl came up to Mike and said, "I just stole second base on you." Mike looked him square in the eye, shook his head, and yelled, "You just stole second base on me? How the fuck did you get on in the first place?" Earl never came out and fucked with Mike again.

Flanny and I were batterymates in the very first game played at Camden Yards in 1992. It was an exhibition game before Rick Sutcliffe came in and pitched the opener against the Cleveland Indians. I remember going to the mound and I said to him, "You know, Mike, this is it for us." He ended up pitching in relief that year for the Orioles. He had an 8.05 ERA in what was to be his final season. It was my final season, too. I quit after playing in eight games.

Mike made his major league debut in 1975 as a 23-year-old and played until he was 40. He finished 167–143 with a 3.90 ERA. Trust me, he was even better than those solid numbers would indicate. The fact that he played 18 years in the big leagues is a testament to just how good Flanny was on the mound.

He was on our special 1983 team. We started off the season pretty well, but we kind of knew it was going to be a tough year for us if we didn't get some pitching help. General manager Hank Peters was keeping an eye down in Triple A ball on Mike Boddicker. He had pitched in a total of 10 games from 1980 to 1982. It was nothing special. He started one game in 1980 and gave up five runs in his debut. He pitched in relief twice in 1981, had seven games out of the bullpen the following year, and then returned in 1983 on May 8 with another stint in relief. Then on May 17, Weaver gave Boddicker a start and he blanked the Chicago White Sox on five hits. That earned him a spot in the rotation.

He was just what the doctor ordered. This kid had great control of all of his pitches, including a big, sweeping curveball, which really kept everybody off balance, and he could spot his fastball almost as good as Palmer. During the whole season, I don't think he shook me off one time. He just wanted to learn the ropes. He did whatever I asked him to do. He was incredible. Mike was 16–8 with a 2.77 ERA and five shutouts. He would have won 20 games if he pitched the whole season; there's no doubt in my mind. He was the MVP of the playoffs that year in our series against the White Sox, pitching a shutout in his only game and striking out 14. For long stretches he was our best pitcher that season.

During spring training of his second year, I told him, "Mike, the league's going to adjust to you. They're going to start looking for your curveball, and you're going to adjust back. So, if you want to take control of your ballgame, it's okay with me. Shake me off and do what you feel is the right thing to do." And that's what he did, and I'm glad. Because whenever you get a pitcher to think ahead to what pitch he wants to throw, you're going to get

100 percent effort. So Bod took control of his own game and in 1984 he was 20–11, led the league with a 2.79 ERA, pitched more than 260 innings, and finished fourth in voting for the AL Cy Young Award. He wanted to go nine innings. He could finish off games as beautifully as anyone.

Boddicker not only had a curveball over the top, but he also could drop down and throw it sidearmed for you, too. He had tremendous flexibility. As I did with Flanny, when we got in a situation when he needed a strikeout or a grounder, I would call for that pitch maybe once or twice a game. It was fun catching him because he had so many pitches in his repertoire.

Mike learned a lot from Palmer, even though Jim was a power pitcher and Boddicker was not. But he could tell Boddicker how to pitch to certain hitters. That's what made that team so great—the camaraderie was excellent. We talked baseball in the locker room before the games and after the game. Bod excelled because he'd listen to Flanny, listen to Palmer, and then implement it in the game.

Boddicker went 79–73 with Baltimore. After he started the 1988 season with a 6–12 record—remember, the Orioles were awful that year—Mike was traded to the Boston Red Sox for Brady Anderson and Curt Schilling. You could say the Orioles got the best of that deal, but Boddicker was 39–22 in two and a half seasons with the Sox.

Another Orioles pitcher, Scott McGregor, was a master at changing speeds and changing his body rhythm. I used to always tease him, telling him he couldn't bruise my hand if I caught him bare-handed. That's an exaggeration, but it really goes a long way toward explaining what kind of pitcher he was.

Scotty has a great temperament. He was very pensive on the mound but in a good way. We had a routine where he would shake off every single pitch and oftentimes would come back to the first one. We did that to throw off the hitter. It was amazing to watch Scotty pitch when he was on his game. It looked like it would be so easy to hit him, but it was really all about his physical and mental control on the mound. He was a lot more intense than a lot of the pitchers I caught, but he had to be that way. Because if he didn't put the ball where he wanted and changed his body rhythm, he probably would have gotten hit hard.

It's incredible how easily he got through some lineups with a fastball in the mid to high 80s. I don't think he got to 90 when he was with the Orioles. But he was reliable guy, a low pitch-count guy. He didn't have that fire on the mound; it was more of a quiet confidence in himself.

Scott spent his entire major league career with Baltimore. He went 13–6 in 1979, 20–8 in 1980, and 13–5 in 1981. He won 14 games in 1982 and was 18–7 in 1983. He could have been MVP of the 1983 World Series, but we lost the first game 2–1 with him on the mound. He threw a five-hitter in the clincher. Scotty won 138 games over his career, but because he didn't have a blazing fastball and played on teams with Palmer, Flanagan, and Boddicker, he probably didn't get the publicity he deserved.

Scotty didn't say too much. He listened and learned. He spoke a lot with Palmer and Flanagan. They all had their own person-alities and different levels of excitement when they were on the mound. Mac was the quiet one. Mike was kind of quiet, too, but was a little more emotional in his ballgames. Scotty would just make it look flat-out easy. That's what was so good about him. He was a pure pitcher rather than just throwing the ball hard and backing it up with a good curveball and a change-up. He controlled the tempo of the game and was great at reading hitters. I thought he was going to be a great major league pitching coach, but he never got to that level on a full-time basis. Scotty was named interim Orioles bullpen coach in late 2013 when Bill Castro was promoted to pitching coach. Scotty is now the pitching coach for the Orioles' Single A affiliate, the Aberdeen IronBirds.

# Chapter 7
## The Iron Man

You can't talk about Cal Ripken Jr. without bringing up The Streak, so let's get that out of the way right now. No one will ever play 2,632 consecutive games again. It's almost inconceivable that Cal would even want to play that many games in a row. But Cal Ripken was indeed the Iron Man, and his streak was a huge part of Orioles baseball in that era.

Playing in Memorial Stadium back in those days really wore on you. To survive it, you had to be in tremendous shape, whether or not you were playing every day. To think that Cal posted for that many games in a row is just incomprehensible. The mental toughness that it took, I don't think anybody can ever match it.

I once said that it helps a player to get a rest every now and then. That statement was not directed at Cal. What I meant by that is that every manager should be cautious of his players. When it seems like they're tired and not producing at the level you expect them to produce, you should be able to give them a day off, a rest from the grind. It's the right thing to do with most players.

To be honest, as The Streak mounted, I think Cal was pretty beat up and hurt and sore. But he didn't feel it because he was just so mentally prepared to be there every day. I mean this about any player, and not just Cal, but if he had gotten a day off here or there, he probably would have been more productive than he was. As it was, he still ended up batting .276 with 3,184 hits, 431 home runs, and 1,695 RBIs and was a first-ballot Hall of Fame entrant in 2007. He was that great of an athlete.

It basically came down to his choice to keep that streak going. People came to see Cal Ripken play. That's what induced the manager to keep him in the lineup. With the exception of 1996 and 1997, the Orioles struggled in the 1990s. The talent wasn't there,

A year after he broke the record for most consecutive games played, Cal Ripken Jr., my former roommate, deftly patrols the infield in 1996. (Baltimore Orioles)

and it was tough to keep fans interested in the team. Attendance started to go down a little bit. But the one guy people kept coming to see was Cal. He was still the best, most productive player on the team.

Toward the end, when there was a year to go before he set the record in 1995, the streak drew a lot of national attention. And you know what? The organization and team and the city needed that.

When he broke the record, I was managing the Norfolk Tides, but I was invited to be at Camden Yards to see the event. I was so happy for him to get there. I was proud of him, proud to have been his roommate for the first three years of his career.

That record was significant around here and everywhere in the world. To stop and think about it, oh my God, that he actually did it is unbelievable. I know how hard it was to go home every night after catching a game because I was dog tired. Earl Weaver wasn't going to let me catch a full season, even though I wanted to. I was mad every time he didn't put me in the lineup. But I couldn't have done it, I know that. There are people who could play every day but not in the major leagues like Cal did.

The reason I thought Cal should be given a rest is that if a player pushes himself too hard, he can get hurt. To not have him available, or on the disabled list, would have really hurt the ballclub because they didn't have a replacement for him at shortstop or in the lineup.

Cal had a unique situation in that his father played a major role in the organization from the time Cal was a kid to when he got into the big leagues. It was a great relationship. Cal Sr. was a minor league manager when Cal was growing up and a coach with the Orioles when his son made it to the majors.

I used to watch Cal when he came out and took batting practice with the team as a high school kid. When he was 16 years old, he hit the ball farther than I did as an adult. He could hit it out in left-center or right-center at Memorial Stadium, which was not an easy park to hit homers in unless you pulled the ball down the lines. But he had that gift of strapping young power. You're born with it. I was watching him in awe, thinking, *Jiminy Christmas, I would have to use a fungo bat from second base to get the damn ball out of the ballpark.*

When he broke into the majors in 1981, Cal had a presence about him from Day One. He was born into the baseball world. He didn't have to learn it when he got into the big leagues. I didn't even know who the Minnesota Twins were when I signed with them in 1967. Cal was around baseball his whole life. When he came to the big leagues, he was a 10-year veteran mentally. Cal was fundamentally sound. He was around his father when Cal Sr. managed in the minor leagues, so he picked up the game as a kid. He knew exactly what he was capable of doing at the major league level before he did it.

Cal Sr. recognized that his son was probably the best player in baseball in the early 1990s. Ken Griffey Jr. was an outstanding player, too, and there were some notable pitchers. But Cal was the best. Cal was the best player in the game, and Eddie Murray was right behind him. Cal was the centerpiece. Eddie was a little bit older and so was I. Eddie and I ended up leaving the Orioles toward the back end of our careers because the Orioles were making changes.

Cal was embedded in that lineup. After many years his stats started to wane a little bit because of the everyday play. But it was still important to have him on the field because everybody in the world was looking at the Iron Man and wondering: was anything ever going to happen to Cal to take him out of the lineup?

There's no doubt that Cal got his grit from his father, who was the toughest coach you ever saw. Senior was fun to be around, but he was a gritty, gnarly guy. His sense of joking around was a bit different. As you were walking in the airport, he would slap you as hard as he could in the chest. He hit me so hard that I would lose my breath. Then he'd just look at you. You knew, in his own way, that he liked you. After he slapped me a few times, I would know it was coming and I put a book under my shirt. Sure enough, he slapped me. And this time I know it hurt him, but he would never show it. He wouldn't even rub his hand.

Cal Jr. was like that, too. He loved wrestling and joking around like that. We had a lot of great times together. We went out to dinner all the time, and he wouldn't hesitate to pick up the check—unlike Tippy Martinez and those guys. I can remember times when Cal sprained his ankle a little bit. He would just tape it up and go out and play. He was as hard-nosed as his father ever was—except he was bigger, stronger, and more talented. I loved having Cal as a roommate because he was so much fun. He was the young guy. I wasn't the young guy anymore. Cal was so big and so fucking strong. Watching him play every day was just amazing.

Cal was such a great athlete and a relentless competitor. Cal was better than anyone at everything he did. You want to play basketball? Cal was outstanding at it. You couldn't budge him, and he played hard defense. He would knock you all over the place, and the elbows would be flying. You want to wrestle with him? Biggest mistake in the world, as I found out. As much as I worked out and as strong as I was, this guy had strength like you couldn't believe. It made you understand why he was such a good player.

Cal had a calm about him that I never had. I was always a hyperactive kind of guy and I think I overdid it. Looking back on my career, I felt like I had to take more batting practice, I had to block more balls, I had to throw more balls. I just didn't leave a stone unturned. Neither did Cal, but he did it without the sense of urgency that I always had.

On the field, Cal redefined what a shortstop should be. There were no shortstops like him in the game when he came in. He was 6'4," as strong as they come, a home-run hitter, a game-changer. You didn't see any shortstops who could even come close to the production level that Cal had.

I played with many a Hall of Fame player, and Cal is surely among the best of them. Certainly, none of them changed the game the way he did—in terms of how you look at the shortstop position now and how it was before he arrived on the scene. He was the precursor to a generation of bigger shortstops like Derek Jeter, Nomar Garciaparra, and Alex Rodriguez. It started with Earl Weaver thinking Cal could play shortstop because he knew the kid could adjust to anything. Cal could have pitched if he wanted. He could do anything.

I thought I worked out a lot. The day I got home from the season, I had a seven-mile run. Then I started my workouts immediately. I lifted free weights and worked out on the Nautilus because I didn't want time to catch up to me. I wanted my baseball career to last forever. I never took any time off during all the years I was in the game. Cal, though, was the only guy I thought matched my work ethic. And maybe he did even more. This guy played basketball over the winter, which was risky at the time, but he never got hurt. Mike Flanagan tore his Achilles tendon playing basketball and missed a year.

Cal loved competition. He would beat you to death wrestling. If he didn't know the game, he would learn to beat you. Cal didn't golf much, but he found a way to be a good golfer. If he wanted to be a professional golfer, there's no doubt in my mind he could have been. He would have found a way to hit the ball farther and better.

I didn't start playing golf until I retired, but I played it religiously until I got pretty good at it. I was a 1-handicap at one time and then fell back to a 3. It was too much work, too much practice for me. But we all got together at Caves Valley outside of Baltimore one day for an outing, and Cal was the captain of one of the teams. He didn't pick me, and I said, "You're going to pay for that, Cal," because the losing team had to buy the other shirts from the pro shop. That day I shot 69, and they had to buy the shirts.

But to see Cal hit a golf ball was something. He didn't play regularly, and golf is a finesse sport. Cal was out there driving the ball somewhere around 280 yards and he never played! He was keeping it on the fairway, too. It was just amazing, but it didn't surprise me that much because he's such a great athlete. I'm sure he could play soccer or hockey if he wanted to.

Cal, perhaps more than anyone, gave back to the fans. He did it early in his career and continued to do so right to the end. Every time Cal came within five feet of a wall, people would ask for his autograph. It was a beautiful thing to see. He accommodated everybody that he could. That was just part of his personality and why people loved him so much. As he was closing in on 2,131 games in a row, he would sign after games, and the line went outside the stadium. People wanted his autograph and a chance to see him close up.

As far as the streak goes, it had to come to an end sometime. Cal was a very smart guy and I think he asked himself, *Where is it going to end and how is it going to end?* Time catches up with everybody, so he started thinking about ending it on his own terms. I'm sure it was a tough decision for him to make because it wasn't only about himself but the Orioles, too. His streak was the most interesting and fascinating aspect of the team. Everybody knew about the Baltimore Orioles because of Cal.

He finally ended the streak by his own choosing before the Orioles' final home game of the season in 1998. He walked into the manager's office and asked that his name be removed from the lineup. How appropriate that the streak would end that way. Not by injury, not because a manager wanted to bench him, but because Cal finally decided it was time.

No one will ever break the streak because no one in today's game will ever want to do that. When they realize what it took for Cal to play in 162 games, year after year after year, they're not going to want any part of it. Sure, everyone wants to hit home runs and have the highest batting average and things like that, but no one wants to make the sacrifice it takes to play every game every year. There's so much money to make in the game today that players will find a way to get their rest after the grind of traveling and playing nine innings day after day. It's the nature of the game now.

It seemed as if Cal had an affinity to do something spectacular in the biggest of games. To no one's surprise, Cal hit a home run in his last All-Star Game. He hit a home run in the game he tied Lou Gehrig's record on September 5, 1995, and he homered again the next night when he broke the record with his 2,131st straight game. He had a knack for getting the biggest hit at the biggest time, and everyone just loved it. Mayors, governors, celebrities, even the president of the United States, came to see Cal Ripken play.

I thought for sure by the end of his career something was going to happen where he just could not make it out onto the field. He played with sprained ankles, sore joints. People would hit him with pitches in the batter's box or on the base paths. But you just couldn't beat him down enough. Mentally, he was just too strong. I thought the wear and tear of playing in Baltimore, along with the heat and humidity, would catch up with him. But he went out there through it all and played every single day. Players in the game today don't want anything to do with that.

In 1992 I came back to the Orioles after spending 1991 with the Milwaukee Brewers. B.J. Surhoff was the starting catcher in Milwaukee, and I was the backup guy to him. At the end of the year, it was time for me to move on. I knew my career was coming close to the end, so I called the Orioles to see if I could try to make the ballclub. Johnny Oates was the manager. It looked like it was going to work out because I had a pretty good spring. I actually made the team, but they needed a week at the beginning of the season to adjust their roster and make it work. Then Chris Hoiles broke his hand, and that opened up a spot for me. I was activated a week into the season, the first year at Camden Yards.

Sometime in June everyone was talking about the streak, even though Cal had a way to go before breaking Gehrig's record. They were talking about how Cal kept rolling along, never got hurt, and played all these games in a row. It seemed kind of funny that it was such a big deal because back when Cal and I were roommates it wasn't unusual for him to play every single game of the season. Besides, in 1992 we had way too far to go before he actually set this record.

After I made the ballclub, I remember they were interviewing me about us being roommates. Cal was in a little bit of a slump, and the interviewer said he might be tired, but they didn't want to take him out of the lineup and everyone was saying that Oates *had* to play him. In response to that, I said, "Well, a manager has to be prepared to take any one of his players out of the lineup when a day off would make him play a lot better." My thought process was that there's no sense in wearing Cal down so that he can be nonproductive when all you have to do is give him a day off once in a while. It would perk him right up. You see Buck Showalter do that now with every one of his players, even the biggest stars. Anyway, after I said that about Cal, I got the feeling somebody took offense to that—at least maybe the way I said it. I didn't mean it in a derogatory sense.

But I think somebody went to Cal and told him that I didn't want him to set the record. That's not the way I said it and that's not what I meant at all. Of course, I wanted to see him set every record there was. I loved the guy. He was probably the best athlete in the game at the time. The only guy who could probably rival him was Bo Jackson. I mean, Cal had so much energy, he was strong, and he played to win all the time.

But in 1992, when I came back, it seemed like it was hard to talk to Cal and pal around the way it was when we were roommates

Cal Ripken Jr. not only recorded 3,184 hits at the plate, but he also was one of the best athletes in the game. (Baltimore Orioles)

and used to play on great teams together. Something happened in the relationship. He was cordial, he would say hello, but it didn't seem the same.

Sure, I was 42, and he was 31. That might have been part of it. But it was a different ballclub in 1992. The young guys on the team kind of banded together and took over that ballclub. Cal and Brady Anderson were like the elite players in the clubhouse. They were very much a part of the whole team, but it just felt like it was about Cal setting the record rather than the Orioles winning. It was unusual because I knew Cal wanted to win as much as anyone. It wasn't really that Cal had changed, but the clubhouse had a different vibe because there were new people around the team at that time. The relationship between me and Cal just cooled off. We used to have so much fun. I don't know, Cal was a mega-star at that time, and I guess I realized it was time for me to get out of baseball, retire, and move on, which I did.

# Chapter 8

# The Lean Years

The Orioles were successful in 1996 and 1997 under Davey Johnson, getting to the playoffs each year. In 1997 they went wire to wire in first place, won the American League East, and then got bounced in the postseason. But the team played well under Davey, who had a keen knowledge of his players and managed the team well.

After the 1997 season, however, Davey and Peter Angelos had a falling-out. Johnson left, and the Orioles hired Ray Miller to manage in 1998, which began a franchise-record run of 14 straight losing seasons—the darkest period in the history of the team.

Ray was a very good pitching coach. He could get these guys to respond to what he had to say; that was a good thing. But at the same time he would come to my side of the fence and tell me how to handle the pitching and what I should do. Back in those days,

Ray Miller, whom the Orioles hired as manager in 1998, comes out to congratulate pitcher Tim Stoddard and me after we won Game 4 of the 1979 World Series. (Baltimore Orioles)

the pitching coach—especially Earl Weaver's pitching coach—had a tough life to live. If a pitcher didn't pitch well for a while, I'm sure Ray paid the price in Earl's office. Earl demanded a lot from his coaching staff, and pitching is the name of the game. At times, Ray probably took a good verbal beating from Earl.

You evaluate the pitching coach on the response from the guys he has to teach and has to handle. Jim Palmer always had rave reviews for Ray, as did Flanagan and Scotty McGregor. Ray had a mantra: "Work fast, change speeds, and throw strikes." That has held true in baseball since the beginning of time and will remain that way. Back then, Earl yelled and screamed at everybody. He had no favorites. Earl told me from the very beginning: "Whenever a pitcher really wants to throw a pitch, let him throw it because he'll give you 100 percent effort and not 50 percent of what you want." But Earl would also say, "I don't want you to throw certain pitches to certain players." So you'd get stuck between a rock and a hard spot, trying to accommodate both Earl and the pitcher looking in for the sign.

Ray knew how Earl wanted things run. He played both sides of the fence. If the pitcher complained about a pitch I called, Ray would tell the pitcher, "You've got to shake him off." And that was the right thing to tell him. But sometimes he would come to me and say, "Ah, this guy just doesn't have it. It doesn't matter what you call." I knew Ray was knocking me to the pitchers, but I didn't mind because he would knock them behind their back to me.

Ray was a very, very good pitching coach. Sometimes a guy knows how to work a staff or run a spring training camp, and he gets promoted to manager. This happens in baseball. But it goes a lot deeper than that. You have to be able to communicate with people. That's why you see more catchers getting managing jobs than any other position. The position revolves around communication with everyone on the field and everyone at every other position. It's almost exhausting. You'd like to go out there and just focus on yourself, how you fit into the puzzle. But when you're a catcher, there's so much that goes through your mind before you call the first pitch.

Anyway, I think it was tough for Ray because you try to be a friend to the guys as a coach. You want to be a friend and you want them to like you. Earl didn't care about that, and that's what made him a good manager. That might have been one of Ray's problems as a manager; he still managed with his heart. That's okay when you're a coach, but it's not okay where you're the manager. He learned a lot from Earl, but it didn't translate during his two years with Baltimore. Ray went 79–83 in 1998 and 78–84 in 1999. Baltimore finished in fourth place both years, and that was that for Ray as the team's manager.

I interviewed for the job in 2000, but the Orioles hired Mike Hargrove. I had no clue how I did in the interview, but I knew right away it wasn't going to happen. The media at that time was not in my corner. They didn't really know much about me and how I managed in the minor leagues with the Los Angeles Dodgers. Peter called Mike and told him he wanted me to be on the staff. Hargrove really took offense to that; he didn't want anyone telling him who his coaches are. He wanted to pick his own guys.

I didn't know Mike at all. I remember the first day he called me up. He said, "Rick, I know you've criticized me before and I don't really want you on my staff." I was shocked because I never talked to Mike in my life and had never even mentioned his name in a sentence. I said, "Well, Mike, I don't think I've ever said anything about you in my life, but you're obviously upset about it. So I'll tell you what I'll do: if you can get that person who said I said something about you, and if he's telling the truth, I promise you I won't take the job because I've never mentioned your name before in my life."

He responded by saying, "Oh, don't worry about it. It was thirdhand information anyway." I said, "Okay, I leave it open to you." And, you know, I was really happy to coach for Mike because he had turned things around with the Cleveland organization and made the Indians a winner.

Unfortunately, we started off on the wrong foot from Day One. He didn't get to pick me, so there was some friction there. It was almost like it was a college hazing deal from the very beginning. We went to Florida for his first spring training with the Orioles, and every morning the coaches got together. They would hold a vote to pick a coach who screwed up or did something wrong the day before, such as saying the wrong thing to a player or messing up a drill. It was supposed to be a fun thing, but it wasn't. Not for me. Whoever got picked received a Mule Dick, which was something long and wrapped in a towel. You had to carry the Mule Dick through the clubhouse. I got it every single day. Every day they voted me the Mule Dick. I laugh at it now because it was almost funny how much Mike did not like me. To this day, I really don't know why. I guess it was that Peter put me in that job, and Mike thought Peter was eventually going to make me the manager. The team was not winning, and I was part of the history of this franchise when we were winners.

There were so many things that went on over the course of that season. Mike spent a lot of time and effort on things that really didn't matter. I would go into the dugout and make sure the clocks were set for batting practice intervals, and he would yell at me in front of the media to embarrass me. It came to a point where I really couldn't do my job as a first-base coach.

I've been close to being deaf ever since I was eight years old. I have 70 percent hearing loss in one ear and 60 percent loss in the other. I had scarlet fever, and the doctor overmedicated me, which destroyed the nerve endings in my ear. Well, I had this watch that my granddaughter gave me. It had an alarm on it with high pitches I don't hear very well. He said to me one day while we were in Boston, "Do you hear that?" I said, "No, what are you talking about?" Then he said, "Your alarm is going off. I'll fix that for you. Give it to me." So I gave him the watch, and he threw it on the floor and hit it with a baseball bat. I should have smacked him right there, but I just felt like being the better man.

Stupid things like that happened all the time. He and his coaches would come to my room at 3:00 AM. They would bang on the door and say, "We think you've got someone in your room. We're running a room check on you." What could I say? I told them it didn't really make sense to run a room check on coaches, but they were welcome to come in and have a look. No one was there, and they knew it, but that's just how life was for me under Hargrove. He was just a very tough guy to deal with. Mike just made life miserable every step of the way. Terry Crowley, my friend, was the hitting coach, and he understood what was going on but couldn't really do anything about it. He just said, "Demps, I know he's being hard on you. He doesn't like you for some reason." I told him I didn't get it either, but I could take all the crap he was going to dish out.

We went to play golf one day. Pitching coach Mark Wiley, myself, third-base coach Tom Trebelhorn, and Mike, who hit a ball across the cart path and near a water hazard. We were all looking for the ball, and as he went around a bush, I saw this bullfrog on a bank. It jumped in the water and startled him. Mike was a big guy, and as he walked around another bush, I yelled, "Gator! Gator!" You never in your life saw something as funny as Mike, as big as he was, jump over that elephant grass in one bound. He ran up the embankment to get away from what he thought was an alligator. Trebelhorn was laughing so hard he nearly fell out of the golf cart, and, to be honest, that might have been the best laugh I ever had in my life. I paid for that dearly the rest of my time there, but it was worth it. My shoes would disappear on getaway day, and I had to wear tennis shoes— which were forbidden by Hargrove—to get on the bus and get on the airplane. I got a verbal spanking from him in front of everybody, something that occurred on a regular basis. My whole time there under Hargrove was just an awful experience. Mike wasn't a bad guy, I just think he didn't want me there because he perceived me to be a threat to his job, which I never would have gotten anyway.

Turns out, he was not the man to get the Orioles back to being successful. Not even close. The team went 74–88 in his first season in 2000, then 63–98, 67–95, and 71–91. Baltimore finished in fourth place every year, just ahead of the awful Tampa Bay Devil Rays. He got fired after the 2003 season, and I interviewed for the job. Peter called me in one day and said, "You're going to manage the Orioles."

I went home, called my wife, and told her I got the job I wanted ever since I retired. She was pretty ecstatic about it. Two days later Peter called me up and said, "Sorry Rick, I've got to renege on that. The two general managers [Jim Beattie and Mike Flanagan] told me that I shouldn't do that. I'm really sorry, but I have to change my mind." I told him, "Peter, don't worry about it. It's okay. I thank you for considering me." They ended up hiring Lee Mazzilli, and I was his first-base coach.

That turned out to be a disaster for the Orioles. They thought they were going to get a part of the New York Yankees history when they hired him, but it just didn't turn out that way. In 2004 Baltimore had a 24–23 record on May 31. Fourteen losses over the next 17 games dropped the record to 27–37, and the team finished 78–84. Next season the Orioles went 16–7 in April and were in first place on June 21 with a 42–28 record. Then they lost 28 of the next 38 games, and the forgettable Mazzilli era ended with him getting fired with the team at 51–56. Sam Perlozzo took over to wrap up a 74–88 season.

The streak of losing seasons continued under Perlozzo and Dave Trembley, who had a connection with president of baseball operations Andy MacPhail from when both were with the Chicago Cubs. So after Perlozzo was fired, Trembley took over on June 18, 2007. Trembley was very good at organizing spring training, so the fact that he could work with young players and he and Andy had a history together worked in Dave's favor. MacPhail just wanted to give him an opportunity over everyone else.

Trembley inherited a team that owned a 29–40 record, following an eight-game losing streak. The Orioles promptly went on a 29–25 tear, and as a result, Trembley had the interim tag removed from his title and was extended through the 2008 season on August 22. On that day, though, the Orioles lost 30–3 to the Texas Rangers to launch a nine-game losing streak.

Before they hired Trembley to be manager, I had thought I might get considered again and that maybe I had a better shot because of my experience. I was very disappointed that I didn't get a better consideration when Mazzilli was made the manager and then Trembley was hired. These guys had no connection to this team whatsoever. They had minor league experience, but so did I.

When it was determined that Trembley couldn't help the Orioles win, I interviewed for the job, and Peter indicated again that I was going to be the manager. Then he called me up a couple of days later, and the same thing happened. He said, "I'm not getting a lot of good response for choosing you and I'm going to have to renege again." That's when I sat down with Peter and said, "Just tell me one thing. Most of the time the GMs are going to tell you they're moving in another direction, that you don't get along with the media well, or that you don't get along with the players very well. Please, just tell me what is it about me that is not appealing to you or the Orioles right now?"

He told me something that I'll never forget, and as a result, I actually left the office feeling good about it. He said, "Rick, I can't hire you—not for those other reasons—but because I can't fire you." And you know what? That made me feel so good about being turned down the other times I interviewed for manager jobs. From that point on, I just let it go. I figured it's never going to happen, so I resolved to be a good coach and enjoy that aspect of the game. Peter eventually offered me the television job with MASN. It was hard for me to come off the field after so many years of being there, but it was a great opportunity for me. I figured that even if I managed at the major league level and won a championship, eventually I wanted to finish up that way, being on TV.

I think it's worth noting that Peter is an incredible person. He's very quiet. He's not in the media like a lot of owners usually are. He's not flashy. You're never going to hear his interviews in the newspapers or TV. But he's one of the best people I've ever met in this game. He has been totally up front with me all the time. If he had something to say to me, he'd call me in the office and say it to my face. I always appreciate the fact that this guy has always been honest with me. It's a shame that a lot of people he hired to run this baseball team have not always been as up front with him as they should be. This organization would have been leap years ahead. I know fans have gotten on Peter for the way he's handled this ballclub, but when you hear the inside story about how all this stuff really went down, about how some people got fired and how some got hired, you really understand why Peter made the decisions he made.

For instance, Peter received a lot of criticism for letting radio announcer Jon Miller go to San Francisco. Peter had asked him to not be so hard on the ballclub. He was always bringing up a lot of negative things. I happen to be one of his favorite guys to rip. If he was telling the truth, I could accept it. But he made stuff up, things like, "Rick Dempsey is hitting .069 with the bases loaded in day games." My family would be kind of embarrassed about that. He never let up. When we did banquets together, he would talk up all the players before introducing them, and when it came to me, he would just smirk and say nothing. *Nothing.* He just took it too far.

Jon was one of the great announcers, but he just had a way about him where he could really shove the knife in and make you look bad in front of the fans. Anyway, Jon deservedly got fired and went to the West Coast, where he belonged. I was fine with him leaving. I never had much respect for him or love for him at all. I don't mind saying that because I said it to his face.

Peter and Mike Flanagan were very close. Mike wanted to get involved in the front office, but he didn't have the education to do the job. So they kept Jim Beattie on board to help Mike. The plan was for Mike to eventually take over as general manager. One of the times I interviewed for the job, Beattie and Flanagan ultimately ended up picking Mazzilli. Peter never told me who talked him out of making me the manager. That was okay. I understood.

# Chapter 9

# The Buck Stops Here

Iinterviewed four times for the Orioles' managerial job, and each time was more frustrating than the last. The last time, when it became obvious the team wasn't going to win under Dave Trembley, I interviewed with executive vice president of baseball operations Andy MacPhail in Peter Angelos' office during the 2010 season. They asked me the same old questions, and I was a little more to the point on how I thought things had to go from that point on. I wanted my own staff and planned to bring back guys like Scotty McGregor as my pitching coach and Rich Dauer as the bench coach. I really had everybody covered, including Terry Crowley as my hitting coach. They were pretty much all ex-Orioles. I'm not sure MacPhail thought that was such a good idea. I thought it was a great idea. It would have been like the New York Yankees, who always seem to bring back players who starred with the organization.

Since taking the managerial job in 2010, Buck Showalter has helped restore "The Oriole Way." (Baltimore Orioles)

But when they finally interviewed Buck Showalter, it was the first time I ever felt like that it was okay if they hired a guy like him instead of me. That's because I had said in every interview that this team can win. They just needed to bring in a good manager who'd been down this road, who'd been in postseason atmospheres, who had survived the wars. None of the previous people they talked about bringing in here over the previous five years had fit. All of a sudden, word got out that Buck was going to be interviewed for the job. I told everyone, "That's the guy that's going to get it. You watch and see."

I was really happy, and when Buck came in and did so well, he proved my point. It seems obvious now, but back then it showed that this team could win if you brought the right person in. I thought at that time I could have done that, but I also knew I couldn't do it as well as Buck did because he had the education at the major league level on how to make these kinds of moves. The game is changing. It's become more statistically based with the shifts and bullpen. There was a transition period, and the Orioles needed someone who was aware of how all of this was going down.

Buck was working as a baseball analyst on TV in 2010, and this job with the Orioles came along at the perfect time. We needed him. This organization needed someone with a solid reputation and the confidence required to guide a winner. We were a very proud franchise going downhill. For so many years, we couldn't even play .500 baseball. We totally lost the fundamentals that Earl Weaver beat into us every day, and that thing called "The Oriole Way" had completely vanished.

Toward that end it makes me sick to see a lot of the pampered players who come into the game today. We went on strike for them so they could make the money they're making today, and they have forgotten us. Do you think any of these players making $20 million would go on strike, give away something like $10 million for the future generation of ballplayers, knowing they wouldn't get any of that money back? No, not in today's game.

Well, after Davey Johnson took the Orioles to the playoffs in two straight years, it was a nightmare for this once-proud franchise. It seemed like fundamentals went out the window, and the players didn't appear as motivated to win. Then Buck came along, and suddenly Baltimore was a contender again.

The thing that separates Buck from many of the other managers in the game is the way he runs the bullpen and the pitching staff. In my mind there's just nobody better at it than Buck. Even though I loved George Steinbrenner, I respected Buck for leaving the Yankees after the 1995 season. He had an established team coming off a 79–65 strike-shortened regular season and he had the best owner as far as buying the talent you needed to win. But George wanted to fire Showalter's coaching staff, so Buck said, "I've got to go, too." That's a tough situation to be in. But Buck made the right call. I knew George could be tough and, though I loved the guy, I didn't have to work for him as a manager. Buck handled it the right way.

So then Buck went to the Arizona Diamondbacks and he won there, too, working with an expansion team that started from scratch. He had two of the best pitchers in the game, Randy Johnson and Curt Schilling, to help him do it. Then Buck went to the Texas Rangers and did pretty well despite having a lack of talent to work with. He didn't make the playoffs during his four years there, but Texas won 89 games in 2004.

When he got here, I was curious to see how he managed. What was the difference between Buck and all the other managers I'd seen? I was hoping that Mike Hargrove was going to be that kind of manager because he came from an organization that was really moving in the right direction, and he dealt with a lot of young guys in Cleveland. I thought, *I'm going to learn something from this guy.* He thought I was there just to take his job. He was the paranoid one, which was his own fault. I learned absolutely nothing from him. It became a tough situation just to make it through the day because everything I did was scrutinized. He made me look bad in front of the players and did stupid things to embarrass me. It was like high school or college hazing. I just bit my tongue until I had enough.

But when Buck came in here, you could tell right away that this guy knew how to win and knew the right way to do it. The players immediately had respect for him, but he did things to earn their respect, too, just by the way he treated them. At that time he proved to be the best manager in the game. I knew he could deal with any situation, and he was going to get players to come here. He was in tune with the minor leagues, so I figured he was going to find the right guys and make this team a winner again. He proved me right. He really did.

I've never had one day of regret at all that he became manager of this team. I've enjoyed watching him manage. I try to think along with him, guessing what he's going to do. That's difficult to do because Buck is not afraid to manage without the book. An example: there was a game in San Francisco on August 14, 2016. The Orioles were winning 8–7 in the bottom of the ninth, and Buck called for Zach Britton to issue an intentional walk to Giants catcher Buster Posey with two outs. That put the tying run at second base and the winning run at first. Buck knew what he was doing because Denard Span hit a grounder to end the game. Buck was looking for a lefty-lefty situation, and it worked. But other managers wouldn't make that move. Buck has balls. That's what I love about him. He has no fear when he makes a move. And he'll back it up. You want to question him on a move? He will tell you exactly why he did what he did. There's no guesswork with that guy.

Buck came here with a reputation as a no-nonsense guy, someone who wouldn't take shit but would dole it out. That's not him at all. It surprised me a little bit, but I think Buck has found a way to change with the game. How do you change with the game and still be yourself? I'm sure he says the things he wants to say to each player—privately. He'll call them into his office and speak his peace. But he will put it in a way where he doesn't embarrass the player nor belittle the player in front of his teammates. Buck leaves it wide open for them to work on the areas where they need improvement.

Another thing is that when you play for Buck, you know where and when you're going to be on the field. That was key for Weaver. Every player knew he had a job on the ballclub. There are some teams where guys don't ever get a chance to play. Believe it or not, I was with the Orioles all season long in 1992, my last year, and I started one fucking game. And Johnny Oates was a good manager. But he didn't handle players the way Buck does. Looking at it from an organizational standpoint, Buck has been everything we had hoped he would be—and more. In his own way, he kind of restored confidence to this franchise again.

There are some comparisons between Buck and Earl. Weaver was tremendously prepared. He was way ahead of his time in terms of incorporating the platoon system and very much into keeping statistics—how hitters fared against right-handers and left-handers in certain situations and against specific pitchers.

Earl brought that into the game before anyone else did. And this is what Buck does. Buck is always prepared to deal with almost everything. He's way ahead of almost every other manager in this regard. He beats the bushes of the minor league system. He knows who the best players are, who's doing well, who's teaching them. He goes so deep to make sure they're getting the kind of work and the attention they need. It pays off at the major league level. Buck just has a great feel for what it takes to win because of his experience and the things he's done with other organizations. He understands how to anticipate the good and the bad and what's going to happen if you don't make good decisions. All of us shake our head at times at whom Buck plays and where he plays them. But you know what? He's usually right.

Here's a great example: you've got a slugger like Adam Jones, a guy who hits tons of home runs, and Buck put him in the leadoff spot early in the 2016 season. Who would have thought that Jones would excel at the top of the order and be the leadoff hitter for the rest of the year? I certainly didn't see that. Buck just wanted to give Adam a different perspective because he was struggling at the beginning of the year. I would have given him three days off, but Buck put him there in the leadoff spot, and he responded with a base hit up the middle on his very first at-bat. All of a sudden, he became the leadoff guy on a team making a run at winning the American League East.

Buck makes good, calculated decisions based on his confidence in himself as a manager. You have to appreciate that because there are so many managers in the game today who are only trying to make the general manager and the owner happy. That's not what good managers are all about. Those guys care about the team on the field and the players in the clubhouse.

Chris Davis was slumping for much of the 2016 season. The shift was taking away a ton of hits, and he struck out a lot. So everyone wondered why Buck didn't take him out of the lineup. Well, Buck is going to stick with the guys he came to the dance with and he's going to do it in a way we may not understand. But the players get it. They understand why they're playing and why they're not playing. There's no question about that.

Now, I believe the Orioles are on the cusp of being a championship organization. Injuries were a factor with this 2016 team, most notably to Jones, set-up man Darren O'Day, and right-hander Chris Tillman. Regardless, I like the potential of this team under Buck, mostly because of its young pitchers.

Dylan Bundy, the fourth overall pick in the 2011 draft, has shown that he's capable of being a Cy Young type of pitcher. Kevin Gausman, the fourth overall pick in 2012, has displayed that type of talent, too. He needs another pitch to work with, but he's a standout starter. I even think that Tyler Wilson, who made his big league debut in 2015, can be taught some things. It's not coming easy to him right now. He needs to learn how to be himself, how to be confident in what he brings to the mound.

This team has strengths that make some people think we should blow all of baseball away. I personally think the Orioles should have brought a five to 10-game lead in the American League East into September. It's not a matter of not having enough talent. But starting pitching, which has long been the strength of this organization, did not fare well.

One thing I really like about Buck is that I can go into his office at any time and talk baseball to him. We both enjoy stories about the old days, and I enjoy picking his brain about what's going on with the team. I could care less about the stuff that the media isn't supposed to hear. That goes in one ear and out the other. But he talks to me about the team and the players, and at least I know I have his respect.

Buck might be the most creative manager I've ever seen in the game. I've played for some really good ones: Billy Martin, Earl Weaver, Tommy Lasorda. That's as good a trio of names as any. But I wish I could have played for Buck and definitely wish I could have coached for him. This guy has no fear. The things I thought I would do as a big league manager were not by the book. Buck is like an image of what was in my mind in the way I wanted to manage a team. But he's taken it to an extreme, even more so. He is just so confident in his players and he instills confidence in them, that they can do just about everything on the field. And Buck gives them that opportunity. How many managers would change a lineup the way Buck has? It's incredible. He puts guys in certain positions, both in the field and in the batting order, and they end up producing. When he makes a lineup—puts in a pitcher or takes one out—not one of those players has any question in his mind as to whether it's the right thing because Buck's proven time and time again that he knows what he's doing. It's been fun watching him.

Probably the biggest find in baseball over the last five years or so has been Britton, who had 47 saves in 47 opportunities and a 0.54 ERA in 2016. When Zach went to spring training in 2011, no one gave him a nickel's worth of a chance to make the ballclub. He was a starter coming out of the minor leagues who simply could not seem to get it together. He didn't have good mechanics at the time. He had all sorts of issues with the physical part of pitching and didn't throw the ball over the plate with any kind of consistency. He just wasn't going to open anybody's eyes.

But he did make the club. Zach was a big, strong kid. Everybody realized that. He went 11–11 in 2011 and in 2012 found himself back in the minor leagues. He pitched in 12 games with Baltimore that season, 11 of them starts, and was unspectacular, going 5–3. It was more of the same in 2013, but the following year was completely different.

Buck decided to see if Britton could be effective as a left-hander out of the bullpen. During that first year, no one ever thought he was going to be a real good closer, but when you needed a lefty for an inning or two, he was there to take that position. Early in 2014 Britton was doing very well in the back end of the bullpen while Tommy Hunter was the closer. Then, out of the blue, Buck gave the closer's job to Britton. Right out of the chute, this kid was throwing incredible innings. He had tremendous velocity, a great sinker. Buck kept calling on him, and he has since developed into probably the best closer I've ever seen in the game.

How can you throw a 97 mph sinker? I caught Orel Hershiser, the pitcher who I thought had the best sinker ever, and he was probably 89, 90 mph with his sinker. But Zach doesn't really throw a sinker in the literal term. His index finger is a lot shorter than his middle finger, and because of that, the ball is really different in its movement as it comes off his fingertips. He still is able to throw it just like a fastball. It's just the way it comes off his hand. It sinks down instead of to one side or the other. It has the movement of a split-finger fastball, but it does it at 97, 98 mph, which has never been heard of in the history of the game. Nobody has ever been able to throw that pitch. So you can tell the hitter that it's coming, and he still can't adjust to it. That's how good it really is.

Over the last five years, I can't think of a single team that has found someone who has had that big of an impact on the game.

He has the physical tools and the pitches to be successful and he's improved in the mental aspect. I've watched him beat a lot of teams, and his reputation for being exceptional at his craft has spread through the major leagues.

But his reputation also included this: at one point he only threw the fastball and the sinker. Sometimes the movement on the sinker is very hard to control. So he started to make adjustments by throwing it up in the strike zone. Unfortunately, by throwing it higher in the strike zone, it flattened out. A lot of guys got chopping base hits off him, and when he was forced to throw the ball up in the strike zone, he started to get hit a little bit more. So, the next adjustment was to come up with a breaking ball.

I go back to two years ago, on June 20, 2014, when Brian McCann of the Yankees came up with the game on the line. Britton didn't throw him anything but a fastball, he brought the pitch up in the strike zone, and McCann got a base hit to get New York to 3–2. Carlos Beltran followed with a three-run homer to win it.

I think that was the turning point for Zach. That's when he realized he had to show batters that he had another pitch. So he came up with the curveball that he has. Well, it's more of a slurve, a cross between a slider and a curve. Because it's so unexpected that he would throw that pitch, almost every hitter takes it. They don't look for it, so they just take it. So all he's got to do is throw it down the middle of the plate. And all of sudden, you don't see those choppers anymore. I don't think I saw one of those kind of hits in 2016.

When he had to come into the strike zone, that's when he had given up his hits.

He got smart. Now he'll throw the slurve, sometimes on the first pitch. Nobody seems to swing at it. And when he throws it with two strikes, they have such a horrible swing that it almost makes you laugh. All of this happened under Buck's watch. You're not going to find a better manager. You can't change the way a great manager does things. But sometimes, there comes a point where it doesn't work in your organization, and you have to start all over. I think that's what happened to Buck when he got fired in Arizona and Texas. Both those organizations knew Buck was set in his ways, so they set out to get someone who was learning his trade and might be willing to make some compromises the other guy can't make.

An example of this is Mike Scioscia in Los Angeles. Mike has done great things with the Angels and he had total support from management. He may not be getting that kind of support anymore. You know how fast people can turn on you in this game. But he's a good manager.

There will come a day when Buck and the Orioles part company, and it is my belief that Buck will walk away on his own terms rather than be fired. Nobody should ever fire Buck Showalter. Of course, Buck understands that Peter might have the last call. He is the owner and he should have the right to make that call. But Peter believes in Buck. And so do I.

Buck did a very good job in 2016. The reason I say that is that he pulled more rabbits out of the hat than anybody I've ever seen in this game. Baseball has gotten so specialized that the whole game really starts after the sixth inning. That's when you start matching up the pitchers against batters, and Buck went most of the season without a balanced bullpen to work with. He only had one left-hander in the bullpen outside of Britton, who is the closer. So Buck had to figure out how to get all those right-handers in the right place at the right time. That takes knowing what the opposing hitters did against every one of them, the history, and all that. If you had no history to work with, then you had to give an opportunity to a young guy, cross your fingers, and hope he pitched well.

That's what happened with Donnie Hart. He was outstanding for us. Hart was taken in the 27th round of the 2013 draft, but the Orioles needed a left-hander in the bullpen in 2016 after getting rid of Brian Matusz. So they brought in Hart, who pitched in 22 games and had an 0.49 ERA, because Buck had faith in him and used him at the right time in games. The kid was one reason why Baltimore made the playoffs.

When you stop and see some of the lineups that Buck came up with, some of the times he sent up a pinch-hitter for guys in certain situations—such as when Hyun Soo Kim hit a pinch-hit

Buck Showalter, who is one of the most creative managers I've ever seen, calls the bullpen in 2016. (Baltimore Orioles)

IF THESE WALLS COULD TALK: BALTIMORE ORIOLES

homer to beat the Toronto Blue Jays late in the year—you've got to give the manager credit for making gutsy, correct calls. I've been around this game longer than Buck has and I've seen some of the greatest managers in this game. I've seen some of the biggest idiots, too. I'd put Buck right up there with the best in today's game and I'd put Earl on top in his era.

Buck is just so well prepared. I know this because I did my share of managing myself. But he did things I'd have never thought of and wouldn't have the balls to try if the idea did come to mind. You've got to have a lot of confidence in yourself to make some of the moves he made. He gave some guys opportunities. Well, I'm just shaking my head thinking of it. And he would come out smelling like a rose. Buck will give a player a chance to prove himself, and most of the time it worked out as a positive for the Orioles. Hart is only one example. Buck never gave up on Ubaldo Jimenez, and though Ubaldo was terrible for most of the year, he came through big in September when the team needed him the most.

Buck got 89 wins out of a team that finished with 19 stolen bases. There was no balance on the team in 2016. It was all power in that lineup. We had some incredible talent, but you've got to remember there are still guys learning to play the game, like Manny Machado and Jonathan Schoop. These guys had statistical swings over the course of the season that were tough to deal with. Schoop was a much better hitter in the first half than the second half. And Manny went through his issues with runners in scoring position. He hit .255 with runners in scoring position and .161 with two outs in that situation. As good a player as Manny is— and I call him one of the top five in the big leagues—he still needs to learn to play the game under pressure. He's got to learn how to adjust like some of the great players I've seen. If you go up there and try to pull the ball all the time and try to hit home runs, you're dead in the water. You aren't going to be a feared offensive player.

It's the same thing with Jones. He's a potential Hall of Fame player, but he goes through these streaks where he makes up his mind to swing at anything close to the strike zone. Sometimes he's successful. But as a leadoff hitter, which really isn't his ideal role, he was only good half the time. You can't be a threat only half the time at the top of the lineup. This isn't a knock on Buck, who got the most out of Jones atop a batting order that really didn't have anyone who would take a walk and get on base consistently.

These guys need to improve their approach so the Orioles can become a team like the Boston Red Sox, who hit for average. They can hit home runs, but you're going to win more games by hitting the ball to the opposite side, bunting when you have to, and having good bat control.

It's very painful to go through a season like this—to show that much power and lead the majors in home runs—and then not get to the finish line. It's almost a mortal sin. These guys have to learn to play the game better. It's not on Buck. It's amazing the team got as far as it did. If it hadn't been for the home runs they got over the last couple of weeks, the Orioles wouldn't have even got into the playoffs.

Earl won his share of games with a three-run homer, but we had guys like Al Bumbry and Dauer who set the table. Cal Ripken Jr. could hit a home run, but he was a better fundamental hitter. He had the right temperament, too. These guys today don't have that yet. Buck can't do everything out there. No manager can. But these are things that have to improve, or we'll never have a World Series champion again. They've got to play more of the one-run style. That

I think Manny Machado, who hit .294 with 37 home runs in 2016, is one of the five best players in the major leagues. (Baltimore Orioles)

doesn't mean you have to get a single. Obviously, there's nothing like a home run. But if you're going to make good solid contact two out of four times, your approach has to be a lot better. If you're up there and you've got a pitcher in the hole, you've got to put the pressure on him. We're still swinging for the fences, no matter what the pitch count. This team could have elevated itself by showing more discipline, but it didn't. We had an incredible first half. The Orioles were 51–36 at the All-Star break and led the AL East by two games. But they were 38–37 the rest of the way and finished third.

In the second half, the Orioles just went up there trying to hit home runs. Their approach at the plate was inconsistent. Manny started swinging at pitches down and away and in the dirt. He's too good for that. But he didn't develop in the second half the way he was supposed to. Neither did Schoop. They had their good games.

But when Schoop really got good at the end, it was because he was taking the ball to center field or to the opposite field in right. And when you're swinging that way, when they hang a pitch, you turn on it. That's what he should have been doing the entire season. He would have had as many RBIs as anyone on the club and somewhere around 30 home runs.

The season ended when the Orioles lost to the Blue Jays 5–2 in the wild-card game. Jimenez got hit hard in the 11th inning while Britton remained in the bullpen, and Buck received a lot of criticism for not going to Zach or Dylan. But really, this team was going to have a difficult tine going the distance anyway. Starting pitching has been a problem for this team for a long time, and this season was no exception. Tillman was definitely the ace of the staff, but even Chris is not a pitcher who goes seven, eight, nine innings consistently. We've lost that in baseball. For whatever reason pitchers don't condition themselves for the late innings. They don't have that kind of stamina. If Tillman lasts only five innings, it's very tough for a manager to figure out who's going to come in next. I mean, he's got great stuff, but he just doesn't go deep in the game often enough.

In the National League wild-card series, I watched Madison Bumgarner go nine innings to beat the New York Mets. Why aren't our pitchers that strong? In my opinion, they don't condition themselves properly in the winter. There's a lot of endurance that has to go into this game. People say you don't have to run. I don't agree with that. Weightlifting is not going to get you over the hump, especially in Baltimore late in the season. Tillman should get to the eighth inning of almost every game. That's the way he should be, but he's not that guy. Bundy and Gausman, they worry me. They're very good, but they also need endurance. They don't have that yet.

They need to be running in the offseason. I never stopped running, and I think that's why I went on the disabled list only three times my entire 27-year career—two times with broken bones and once late in my career when I did something stupid and strained my back.

This team can win the World Series. But it has to be better. The pitchers have to go deeper in games. We've got to learn a way to cut down the number of pitches that are thrown. Our catchers need to be better at framing pitches. Getting our pitchers deeper in games has a lot to do with what our catchers do. Matt Wieters and Caleb Joseph are good but don't set up well, and I don't mind saying that. And we don't consistently give good targets. We've got a lot of adjustments to make. The pitchers have to become more durable so we can turn the game over to O'Day, Brad Brach, and Britton. It can happen. The only complete game the Orioles had all year was by Ubaldo, and if he can do it, anyone can.

This team has as much talent, pitching-wise, as any team in the AL East. But they didn't blossom the way they were supposed to. They came on at the end, but they should be a lot further ahead than they are. Gausman's had enough experience that he should be one of the dominating right-handers in the game. He should be somebody you know is going to go at least seven innings every time out. He's that good. His breaking ball got better toward the end of the season, and his split-finger change-up was incredibly good. Now, learn how to use it. This team needs to rely on pitching more than power. And the Orioles shouldn't count on the home run to win. The hitters on this team need better at-bats with runners in scoring position. You need to get singles sometimes, too. They've got to make some serious adjustments if Buck is going to get this franchise to the finish line.

# Chapter 10

# Sharing the Knowledge

**M**y first taste of managing came in the 1970s when I was a player/manager in winter ball in Puerto Rico. I had a guy named Mike Dupree as my closer. He was a hothead. Every time I brought him in—even if we were up by five runs—he'd lose the game. So, as he was in the process of blowing another game, I went to the mound to pull him. I said something to Dupree, he got upset with me, and he threw his glove at me. It grazed my face. I went right at him on the mound and knocked him out with one punch. I got a standing ovation. I looked at my buddy, Pete LaCock, who came running from first base and said, "I think I fucking killed him." And LaCock said, "Ah, fuck it, let him die." They took him to the hospital, and it turns out I broke his jaw, which ended his winter baseball season.

So now I had to tell his wife. She lived right underneath me in our condo building. I knocked on the door, she answered, and I said, "I've got good news and bad news for you." She said, "What's the bad news?" I said, "Well, I got into a little scuffle with your husband and I hit him and I broke his jaw and he's in the hospital right now getting fixed up. I'm sorry." Then, of course, she said, "What's the good news?" And I answered, "You're going to be home for Christmas."

\* \* \*

My final year as a major league player was in 1992. I was 42 and back with the Baltimore Orioles. I felt like I could still play, but I didn't get much playing time. I was on the roster for quite a while, but I only started one game. I guess that was the writing on the wall. I only got nine at-bats in a whole season. Toward the end of the season, right before the September call-ups, Chris Hoiles

With my postseason experience being just one of the many things I gleaned from my 24 years in the big leagues, here I meet with manager Joe Altobelli and pitcher Storm Davis during the 1983 World Series. (Baltimore Orioles)

returned to health, and Mark Parent became the backup. They took me off the roster. Then, they put me back for September.

At the end of the year, I had a meeting with Johnny Oates and general manager Roland Hemond, but they just wanted other people coming in. I felt like they really didn't want me there. I was a little bit upset about it because I didn't get a chance to play and prove myself.

After deciding to retire in '93, I was waiting to hear back from the front office about managing in the minor league system. Evidently, they weren't too serious about it. They wanted me to meet with them about where they were going to place me in the organization. So I was there for the meeting, but they didn't even show up. Doug Melvin was in charge at that time and he didn't even give me the courtesy of discussing the possibility of me landing a job with the team. I figured if it wasn't important enough for him to at least call me and tell me he wasn't going to be there, they had no clue what they wanted to do with me—if anything.

Fred Claire of the Los Angeles Dodgers, however, was calling me on a daily basis to find out my plans. He wanted me for L.A., so I just decided to go in that direction because those people wanted me there. I had spent some good years as a player with that organization. In 1988 we won the World Series there, and Claire and I developed a solid friendship. When I left he told me that when I was ready to shut it down that I could get a job managing within the Dodgers' system. My loyalty still was with the Orioles, but I didn't feel as if they wanted me. They had a whole new regime of people who weren't part of the good years when I was playing here. That part of Orioles history was going downhill quickly, and it showed in the won-lost record.

So I went to the Dodgers. I managed in Class A Bakersfield my first year in 1993. That was an eye-opener for me because I tried to be like Earl Weaver. You know what? I was awful. I was terrible. I admit it. I just wasn't myself. I was yelling and screaming at kids when they couldn't do the simple things. That's what they're in A ball for—to learn the simple things from the start. I just could never accept losing at any level. During my first spring training as an A ball manager, we won every game. Then when our team started the season, we had a tough time winning any game. We were just a very, very young team in the California League. Most of those teams had major league players rehabbing there because they belonged to teams that played on the West Coast. So we ended up going against players who were so much more advanced than the kids I was trying to teach how to play. I yelled at those kids because I figured that was the way managers have to do it. It just didn't work in that era. I wouldn't call that first year a success. But it did teach me that I needed to just be myself and try to teach people the game the way I learned it.

Claire realized it was tough for me at first, but he still came to me and offered me a Triple A managing job the next year. He said, "You know something? You've got to try to be yourself. You can't be Earl Weaver, kicking dirt on the plate." He was right. I was a complete idiot. I was almost embarrassed at the end of the season.

Claire put me in charge of players who were a little more advanced. In 1994 I was more myself around the players, and we won the Pacific Coast League title. We worked hard and we spent extra hours on the field developing these guys for playing at the major league level. But at the same time, we had good times together. These kids could play. I didn't let them step out of line, nor did they want to step out of line. Triple A ball is tough because players' agents are getting more involved in how their clients are being used—where they are in the batting order, how much playing time they get, what you're doing with them in the field.

I would get a call on the phone, and an agent would say something like, "I want my guy batting third in the lineup. There's no way he should be batting sixth." I thought at the time that agents were ruining the game of baseball because they demanded so much, especially when a good player was wanted by an organization. The agent wanted to control everything about him, and I resisted. I had battles on the phone, telling these guys, "You're not going to tell me where to put a player in the lineup. You need to talk to the general manager or the minor league director. You don't need to call me on the phone. And don't call back!"

In spite of this, we had a great year in 1994. After the baseball season, Dodgers manager Tommy Lasorda had a minor heart attack. The media started talking about who was going to be his replacement. He was the biggest name in Dodgers baseball at that time. Some of the media people I got close to in L.A. said, "Dempsey would be a good pick. He won the PCL title and can obviously manage a team." The farm director, Charlie Blaney, immediately called me on the phone and said, "Don't ever think that you're going to get the job managing the Dodgers. Forget it." That came right out of the blue, and I'm not talking about Dodger Blue.

So at that point, I felt like this wasn't the place for me. I didn't have a future here. I decided to move on and I got a job in 1995 as advance scout for the Colorado Rockies, which was quite an education. Anyone who wants to manage should have to be an advance scout first, to see how the whole system works. It was a lot of nights traveling, going to all the different cities ahead of the team. You get in at 2:00 AM and just write reports on everybody until the sun comes up. You get three or four hours of sleep and do it all again. It was a rough, rough year. Along the way I met Jack Zduriencik, the minor league director for the New York Mets. I told him that I would like to get back on the field, and he asked if I would manage the Norfolk Tides, the Mets' Triple A affiliate, in 1997. And I did.

I went through a real good run with the Tides for two years. That was fun, too. We had a lot of good players. I remember my first spring training there with the Mets that this big catcher named Todd Pratt was trying out. He had taken a year off and was coming back into pro ball. I remember being introduced to him. He said, "Mr. Dempsey, it's so nice meeting you. I hope I can just make your team as a backup catcher." And I said to him: "Listen, if you want to work extra, I'd be happy to come out here and work with you. But if all you want to be is a backup catcher in Triple A ball, don't show up tomorrow. If you want to be a major league player, be here at 8:30 in the morning on the field." He almost started crying because he thought I was mad at him.

Well, Pratt ended up being the best player on my team. He ran the ballclub, which was beautiful. He was the hardest worker out there. I had Charlie Greene, who was a 40-man roster player, and I just knew Greene was never going to hit enough to be a major league player. Todd wasn't as good a catcher, but he was working at it. And he was a big, strong hitter, sort of in the mold

171

of current Orioles star Chris Davis. He was that strong. He was that player on the team who made everything work. He would get on the other players when they didn't hustle. He did my job for me. That's exactly what you want, having the core of the team police themselves. And these guys stayed in contention all the way to the last day of the season. The Mets said they didn't like any of my players, but they ended up taking almost half the team. Benny Agbayani made an impact with the Mets. Cory Lidle, who died in 2006 when he crashed a small airplane into a building in New York City, was also a stud. The Mets took my entire pitching staff. And Pratt ended up making it to the big leagues. He hit a big home run in the 1999 playoffs to help the Mets beat the Arizona Diamondbacks in the final game of the National League Championship Series.

Todd went to big league camp the next year and loved talking about how much fun it was to play under me at Triple A ball and how I resurrected his career. The feeling was mutual. Bobby Valentine, the manager of the Mets, cut him. Pratt, the big old guy, was in tears. I told him, "Todd, you're going to have to learn how to evaluate the people who are evaluating you. Your loyalty needs to be with the man who's managing that ballclub. You don't go up to him and tell him how great the guy is who wants his job."

Valentine rarely talked to me. We had minor league organizational meetings all the time, but Bobby was never involved in that. So, my two-year contract ended after the 1998 season, and I didn't get rehired by Jim Duquette. The reason, I believe, is that I fought those agents tooth and nail. Heck, players themselves came up to me and said, "I need to hit second" or "I need to hit third." I said, "When the farm director comes up and tells me where you need to hit, I'll do it. Until then, you'll hit where I want you to hit or you can sit on the bench."

There were other problems while I was in Norfolk. Brent Bowers, who eventually became an Oriole, got mad at me because I didn't go to the official scorer to get a ruling changed. He hit a chopper to the pitcher, who double-pumped and threw it down the right-field line. He wanted me to get him a base hit. I said it wasn't a hit, and there's no sense in me going to the official scorer. The kid got so mad that he grabbed his bat and started slamming the bat rack. Then he threw the bat full-speed down the middle of the dugout. He almost hit five or six guys. So I told him to pack his bags, basically threw him off the team without the Mets' permission. I think that's another thing that cost me my job with the Mets.

During that 1998 season, Davey Johnson was looking at some of my players. He had a scouting job at the time. He said he may have an opportunity to manage the Dodgers. We had been friends for a long time, we played some golf together. He basically got me hired as a coach with the Dodgers in 1999, and I stayed through 2000. When Davey got fired, I went with him.

I interviewed for the Dodgers job and came in second to Jim Tracy. I came back east and took the Comcast job, covering the Orioles. That was kind of fun, doing a show with Kevin Kiley on television. Then Eddie Murray left the Orioles, and I talked with Peter Angelos about coming on board as a coach in 2002. That led to my lamentable tenure under Mike Hargrove.

\* \* \*

Much of what I learned about baseball came from conversations I had with Cy Young winners like Jim Kaat, Dean Chance, and Jim Perry in 1969. I'd go back to my hotel and write down everything. I learned how to receive balls and things like that from guys like Bob Rodgers, a catcher for the Minnesota Twins. He would tell me how to use my soft hands and how to frame pitches. They don't teach those things nowadays in baseball. They don't really show a catcher how to frame a pitch properly, where to sit behind the plate, how close to be to the hitter. You just don't hear anything about those things from instructors in the minor leagues anymore. It's so important where a catcher sets up behind the plate. Ninety percent of all catchers in the game today sit so far back that by the time the ball gets over the plate and lands in their glove, it's so far out of the strike zone that trying to frame the pitch isn't going to get you the call on a close one.

You've got to stay up so close that you can almost touch the back leg of the hitter in the batter's box. When you reach out and catch the ball, it's got to be so close to the plate that you're only inches from getting hit by the swing. You can go a whole season without ever getting your glove tipped by a bat if you do it properly. Then you're going to get so many more pitches—probably 15 percent—called strikes. And that's important when you end up catching 200 pitches a game from your starter and your bullpen. That's 30 more strikes and 30 fewer balls. And that means a whole lot more 2–2 counts, which is a pitcher's count, rather than 3–1 counts, which is a hitter's count. You're going to end up losing more ballgames when you get in those latter situations.

You learn little things like that, and it carries through your career. I took all that with me to Baltimore, and I enhanced my knowledge by talking to a pitcher like Jim Palmer. It all started to open up to me when I got here to Baltimore and got to talk to some of the better pitchers in baseball. Sometimes I would even sneak some questions to guys who weren't even on my team. Mel Stottlemyre and Catfish Hunter, I talked to them when I was with the New York Yankees and maintained that bond after I left. As time goes by, if you can stay healthy yourself and stick around, that kind of information is invaluable. You try to give it to today's players, but they don't really care to listen. You want to talk about game philosophy and how you can help get them into the seventh inning with your starter, but they don't want to hear it.

When I managed in the Dodgers organization and they had young, talented pitchers come in, they would have pitch counts even in Triple A baseball. I said, "If you're going to put them on a pitch count, why not put them in a four-man rotation?" They looked at me like I had an eye in the middle of my head, like I was a Cyclops or something. They thought I was crazy, but the way a pitcher gets better is to have that ball in his hand and to get a feel for it as often as he possibly could pitch in the minor leagues. Sure, when you get to the major league level, go to a five-man rotation, but when you're on a pitch count, you need to throw more often. A lot of these kids would get to the big leagues a lot quicker and be more effective after they learned how to throw a curveball or a change-up on a more regular basis. They wanted to go to a six-man rotation, and I couldn't believe it. By the time the kid got the ball back, he'd forgotten how to throw. It was too long. There was some validity to what I was saying, but because I wasn't raised in the Dodgers organization, they didn't want to listen to me.

When I was with the Orioles, our pitchers knew what to do when behind in the count. In those situations, it wasn't, "How can I strike this guy out? How can I get him to pop up?" No, you looked at it as, where do you want him to hit the ball? The answer was on the ground, the opposite way. That's how you have to think. So you throw him the toughest pitch to put in play, which is still—and always will be—the fastball down and away. Guys like Palmer, Mike Flanagan, and Mike Boddicker had command of that pitch. When they didn't, they got beat. That didn't happen often. They mixed it up on occasion, but I'd say 85 percent of the time they're going with a fastball down and away to try to get back in the count or let the hitter get himself out. Even if it's a base hit, that's the least amount of damage it could do. More often than not, we were more successful because we didn't let them pull the ball and hit it out of the ballpark. When hitters are at 3–1 or 2–0, they're looking for a fastball to drive. The way it is in baseball today, a lot of pitchers try to use an inside fastball in that situation. That's a huge mistake because if you miss inside by one inch, you walk the batter. If you get it over the plate, they can hit it out.

* * *

In my first spring training with the Minnesota Twins, teams would send seven guys on a road trip to play in sort of a spring training pickup game. The idea was to give pitchers a chance to start so they could stretch their innings, leading up to the opener. In this particular instance, the Chicago White Sox, the Houston Astros, and the Baltimore Orioles all sent players to Winter Haven to face the Boston Red Sox. I ended up catching Wilbur

Wood, one of the best knuckleballers in the game. It was my first experience at catching a guy who had a good knuckleball. It wasn't all that tough. I was quick on my feet and could cover some ground. I had on a regular catcher's mitt, and when the ball fluttered a lot, I just knocked it down and got in front of it. Well, on this day Wilbur got wild low. So he walked the first three guys of the inning, and the bases were loaded. I went out to the mound and said, "Wilbur, you're low on every pitch. The ump isn't giving you that pitch. You've got to bring it up a little." That's what he did, and it was sailing all over the place. I had three passed balls in a row. Three runs came in, and then the batter hit a home run. When he got to the plate, he said, "You cost me a grand slam, rookie."

As it turned out, I got such a good look at Wilbur, it helped me hit the knuckleball. I went 6-for-12 against Wood after I joined the Orioles. As Harmon Killebrew told me, you have to move up in the batter's box. You try to get the ball before it breaks. You always looked for them to throw the fastball on a 3–1 count. Most knuckleballers will give you a nice cherry to hit.

I never got to be a major league manager, but I learned plenty from being a catcher in the big leagues. I loved talking baseball with Jim Palmer, Mike Cuellar, Pat Dobson, all the good ones. I wanted to find out what made them good and what I could do to make them pitch even better. I think catchers in today's game have forgotten how important it is to build that kind of rapport with the pitching staff. They just don't do that sort of thing. They don't communicate enough. That's why you see the position deteriorating. There are so many simple little things they need to do that they probably never heard about.

I catch a pop-up in the 1979 World Series. I always prided myself on my fielding range. (Baltimore Orioles)

There are a thousand things you've got to understand before you even set up behind the plate in a big league game and handle a pitching staff, like how to block a ball, throw a ball, frame a pitch, go after a pop-up, check your defense, read the hitters coming up, and on top of that, you've got to read the pitchers you've got on the mound. Then you have to understand the situation and think three batters ahead all the time.

You might think you need a four-year education in college to understand what it means to be a good defensive catcher. You don't. All it takes is a willingness to do what it takes to play your position and help your pitcher. The first thing you do when you walk out on the field is grab some chalk on the baseline, throw it up in the air, and see which way the wind is blowing behind the plate. Then you look at the flags in center field. If the flag is blowing straight in and the chalk you had in your hand goes toward the pitcher, you know you'll be dealing with a swirling wind. So don't go back too far when the ball gets popped behind the plate. You put that thought in your mind.

Long before the first guy steps to the plate, you've done your homework. You've talked with the manager, the pitching coach, and the pitcher and you know what pitch your guy likes and what pitch you think will get the batter out. You know the pitcher's strength and you know the hitter's weakness. Multiply that by the game situation and divide by the count, and hopefully you've found the answer you're looking for.

There's a lot to it, but you learn while catching a pitcher in the bullpen and seeing his release point. How big is his curveball? If a guy has a break that's a foot and a half, do you want to give the target right at the knees so that it comes through the strike zone a foot and a half above your glove? No, you want to give a target a foot and a half below the knees, so that when it reaches the height of its break it barely touches the strike zone, and then it drops out of the strike zone. Those are the kind of things you've got to know.

Do you soft-hand a ball through the strike zone? No, you don't. That's one of the biggest fallacies of the game as far as catchers receiving a ball. You don't absorb the pitch. You reach out, catch it, and bend it back toward the strike zone with your wrist. You give that umpire a chance to call it a strike. He wants to call it a strike. He wants to have a quick game. He wants to go home quickly. He's seen a million freaking baseball games and wants this one to be quick and sharp with no indecision and people yelling at him about balls on the corner that the catcher didn't make look like a strike.

In my day, if you dropped a ball—regardless if the pitch was right down the middle—veteran umpires like Nestor Chylak would call it a ball because you didn't do it right. So you would learn to discipline yourself and you didn't ever drop a ball. You didn't miss a ball that bounced in front of the plate. I don't care if it was a fastball or a curve. People in today's game say, "You don't block fastballs." Well, you'd better block a fastball in my day or you're back in the minors working at it. You've got to expect every single pitch to be in the dirt so you can adjust accordingly. Before you set up, you've got to anticipate it. If it's two strikes on the hitter, you ain't letting it get by you. You're not letting the guy get to first base on an easy ball to block. You've got an area—an arm's distance to your left and to your right—that you've got to cover. Nothing gets through it. Unless it bounces over your head, you are not letting it get by you.

I used to tell Steve Stone with two strikes, "I want this ball in the dirt. Drop this thing a couple feet in front of the plate, he'll swing and miss, I'll block it, and we'll get the out." He tried it a few times and I never missed it—I mean, never—because he had faith I was going to do it. He won 25 ballgames with that approach. I don't know how many catchers ever went to their pitcher and said, "I want this ball in the dirt." He knew I wasn't going to let him down.

Early in my career, I was never really good at blocking a ball. I kind of developed that talent on my own. I learned to be quick on my feet and still stay low in the strike zone. I almost had to be as strong as a ballet dancer, balancing on my toes and getting off my feet quickly. Both feet have to work together, and you have to maintain your balance. I would learn how to bat a ball with my shoulder and keep it in front of me. It was very tough to get to second base on me because I tried to block the plate better than anyone in the game. It worked, too. I finished my career with only 61 passed balls in 1,633 games over 24 years.

# Chapter 11

# The Best of the Best

Choosing the best Orioles of all time, position by position, is mostly opinion, but one part is obvious. Who is the best shortstop? Yeah, Cal Ripken Jr. But choosing the best second baseman, best catcher? Not so easy. Here are my thoughts:

**CATCHER**: Probably the most productive catcher the Orioles ever had from an offensive standpoint was **Gus Triandos**. He was well respected throughout all of baseball as one of the best power hitters at that position. So you'd have to give him a bit of an edge in that respect.

Gus played eight seasons with the Orioles—and like me—started his career with the New York Yankees. He was a three-time All-Star and hit 30 home runs in 1958. I don't know if they kept defensive statistics in those days and I really don't know how well he did in calling a game, blocking balls behind the plate, and throwing out runners. But when I came here, the big name in catching historically was Gus. They named streets after him in Maryland. That should tell you enough about how much people really loved him in this city.

When I came along in 1976, I only had to look back a very short distance to see **Elrod Hendricks** and **Andy Etchebarren** and how they platooned at that position behind home plate. Digging into how this ballclub became the best organization in all of baseball, the catchers and how they handled the pitching staff was as significant as anything else. I mean, we're talking about four 20-game winners. I wasn't here in 1971 when Dave McNally, Mike Cuellar, Pat Dobson, and Jim Palmer all won 20. But I caught Palmer and Cuellar and Dobson. The only one I didn't catch was McNally, who was gone by the time I got here.

The work of Elrod Hendricks and Andy Etchebarren behind the plate is a major reason why Dave McNally, Mike Cuellar, Jim Palmer, and Pat Dobson each won at least 20 games in 1971. (Baltimore Orioles)

There was so much to learn about those pitchers and how they put a gameplan together. It was imperative for me to come here and find out just how to read those kind of pitchers and learn to read hitters and then put those facts together to form a plan of how to pitch a game with that guy standing on the mound.

Catching was a huge part of the game, and I was able to listen to Etchebarren and Hendricks. They were the guys who made the Orioles great. Etchebarren played a few games with the Orioles back in 1962 and stuck with them from 1965 to 1975. He never hit more than 11 home runs in a season and batted as high as .270 just once in 1971. Elrod played from 1968 to 1979 in Baltimore and was okay with the bat. But both those guys were solid behind the plate and knew how to work hand-in-hand with the pitching staff. When I came along, there were some things I could do a little bit better physically than Etch and Elrod. I could throw, I could block balls, I was very quick behind the plate. I could pick guys off the base that looked at me cross-eyed.

We had great plays for getting the extra outs on the bases. I didn't match Etchebarren or Hendricks at the time, but I had a great teacher in Cal Ripken Sr. He understood catching better than anybody in the game. I know from sitting in the dugout as a coach how hard it is to see what's going on. You've got to watch where a catcher moves—inside, outside, up, or down. I'd look over at Cal—he had that unmistakable whistle—and knew what he was talking about when he said sit down, get down lower. He meant below the strike zone. Senior taught me how to move the glove to help the pitcher find a release point. Learning from Cal all those years about how to help pitchers be better is probably why my standard for catchers is so high.

I was with the Orioles for 12 years as a catcher, and we went through some pretty good streaks together. I don't think Andy and Elrod or even Triandos were as outspoken as I was at the time. I pushed guys. I yelled and I screamed. They probably got tired of listening to me and I'm sure there were times when they considered me to be very annoying. But we took winning to another level.

They took a vote of the fans before we closed down Memorial Stadium in 1991, and I was picked as the Orioles' best catcher of all time. That's probably because I had so much interaction with the fans. I probably didn't deserve it. Defensively, maybe. Also, I was very lucky that when I caught for the Orioles, no team won more games over those 12 years. I'm very proud of that.

**PITCHER**: **Jim Palmer** was the best pitcher the Orioles ever had. Other pitchers had some good runs, but Jim was a perfectionist. That's what made him so valuable when he started talking to other pitchers on the staff. He was an encyclopedia when it came to what it takes to be a winning pitcher. This guy wanted to go nine innings every time out; he was not going to turn the game over to anybody in the bullpen to mess up a win he could get. That's what it was all about with him, completing those nine innings or even more if he had to.

Palmer looked at every single hitter differently. He never gave up a grand slam. He knew the guys who could ruin that distinction for him, so he pitched around them when the bases were loaded. He was that smart. He thought that far ahead in those kinds of situations.

**FIRST BASE**: That's a tough pick. **Eddie Murray** was one of the greatest clutch hitters in the game. As far as batting average, you wouldn't say he was the best hitting first baseman around, but he certainly was the most productive and most dangerous. When the game was on the line, you'd definitely want Eddie standing up there because his approach to hitting was unlike anyone I'd ever seen. You'd watch him take batting practice and you'd want to puke. He'd flip at the ball and barely hit it through the infield, but come game time, when he had to go down and get a tough pitch, he would get it. Everything just fell into place for him.

**Boog Powell** was also solid at first base. I never even knew who Boog was until I got to the big leagues at 19 years old with the

Minnesota Twins. I heard there was this really, really big human being, bigger than any two people in the game. He was listed at 6'4", 230 pounds. That's a laugh. Heck, he probably weighed 250 in high school. When I saw Boog for the first time, I think his left leg weighed more than my weight at the time of 145 pounds. You want to talk about a character in the game. Eddie eventually took over as the Orioles' most notable first baseman, but Boog in his day was an incredible hitter and a tremendous defensive player. He was American League MVP in 1970 and deservedly so. He played in 154 games and batted .297 with 35 homers, 114 RBIs, and 104 walks. The guy swung for the fences and still managed to have a .412 on-base percentage that season.

Oh, and Boog is one of the nicest guys you'd ever want to meet, so down to earth. I truly understand why people in the state of Maryland love him so much and remember all that he did. He fit right in with Frank Robinson, Brooks Robinson, and the great players we had here. The magnitude of what Boog did was formidable, but perhaps he was overshadowed by Frank and Brooks.

These days, Orioles fans get to see another big-time slugger at first base, **Chris Davis**. He's in a world of his own. Eddie and Boog, they were probably better technical hitters. They didn't strike out as much. They had a better fundamental idea about hitting. But as long as I've been alive, I've only seen two guys in the game who just mesmerize you when they made contact with the baseball. That's Chris and Harmon Killebrew.

When Chris hits the ball, it goes so high you wonder if and when it's ever going to come down. Killebrew did the same thing. He would hit 'em nine miles high. It's part of the uppercut these guys have. Davis is stronger than anybody I've ever seen in the game. He may not hit the longest home runs, but he certainly hits the highest, most impressive home runs. When he makes solid contact, anything can happen. I've seen him hit one to the opposite field in left, and he's shaking his head because he didn't get all of it. But it ends up going two rows deep. He has that type of strength, which I don't think I've ever seen from anybody in this game. He's fun to watch when he gets rocking and rolling because everything he hits is just a rocket. I've always had an affinity for watching the strong players. I always wanted to be that guy myself, someone who could just walk up to the plate and make contact and see it fly 40, 50 rows deep. I wanted to do that so bad.

I wished I could take a pill that would make me a home-run hitter. I was deep into my career when I found out, yeah, *there is* a pill you could have taken. But by that time, it was way too late to start experimenting with steroids or something like that. I've never taken a drug in my life, so I guess it wouldn't have happened anyway—even if I had it available to me when I was a player.

**SECOND BASE**: I didn't play with **Roberto Alomar**, and he only spent three seasons with the Orioles. But during that time they reached the playoffs twice. In 1996 he hit 22 homers and had 94 RBIs. In 1997 he batted .333 and in 1998 he played in 147 games and hit .282.

But defense was his calling card. This guy did everything defensively with flair. I saw him as a little kid, hanging around the batting cage when I was with the Yankees, because his father, Sandy, was an infielder with us at that time. Robbie was always playing catch with his brother and the next thing you know he's a major league player. As years went by, he established himself as the best second baseman in the game. Alomar put up tremendous numbers and on July 24, 2011, he was inducted into the Hall of Fame.

**Davey Johnson** certainly puts himself up there among the best Orioles at the position. I never thought he was as big and strong as those guys who hit the big home runs. But you look at the numbers he put up, and the man could hit the ball. He hit 66 home runs in eight years with Baltimore and then went to Atlanta in 1973 and banged out 43 homers in his first season with the Braves.

I'll tell you though, Baltimore's current second baseman, **Jonathan Schoop**, has more potential than anyone I've ever seen and I've seen Robinson Cano for years. Schoop has a discipline about him that Cano has never had. Schoop has a feel for the game that's better than Cano. I think that's because Cano is so good; he just gets bored with the game and doesn't hustle all the time. Maybe he takes advantage of his own talent and thinks he can be sloppy and throw the ball the way he wants to. He never has been totally disciplined and totally committed to the game, even though he's super talented and I love the kid. If someone had just worked with him to hone his skills, this guy would be astronomical in his statistics and as an all-around player. But I see Schoop moving up the ladder, and he just might become the best second baseman the Orioles have ever had. He has the right attitude right now.

**SHORTSTOP**: From a defensive standpoint, **Mark Belanger** and **Cal Ripken** were two different kinds of infielders. All around, though, it's not even close. Cal is the best shortstop the Orioles have ever had. Cal was a thinking infielder. He got that pretty much from his father. That's what Cal Sr. instilled in me: think the position. Think about evaluating pitchers and hitters and then put the scenario together. Cal Jr. was methodical about how he thought the shortstop position should be played. He knew he didn't have the best range of any shortstop; he wasn't like an Ozzie Smith who could go get the ball and make an acrobatic play. Cal stayed within his own ability and he was perfect with what he had. He knew how to cut a corner.

You can see how good Cal really was by watching **J.J. Hardy**. J.J. will cut a ground ball off because he knows that's as much as he can give with his ability to get the ball to first base. That's why you see him cut across the infield and short-hop balls. Cal did that as well as anybody in the game. He also changed the face of the game because nobody figured a guy as big as Cal could play shortstop. You knew he could play third base, and he eventually ended up there. But at shortstop he was incredibly adept at turning a double play, slapping the tag on runners trying to steal, and covering a lot

Manny Machado has the potential to become an even better third baseman than the great Brooks Robinson. (Baltimore Orioles)

of territory. Cal proved to everybody that, even though he wasn't a particularly fast guy, he could play the position as well as anybody—heck, better than anybody.

**THIRD BASE**: That's got to be **Brooks Robinson**. But hot on Brooksie's tail is **Manny Machado**. You don't see guys like this come along every day. Every couple of decades you see a guy like Manny, who's got the potential to be a better third baseman—if there's such a thing—than Brooks Robinson was. Brooks just wrote the book on how to field the position. He would keep his head behind the ball, and no one charged a slow roller better than him. Brooksie didn't have a lot of speed, but like Cal he had a knack for cutting off ground balls and knowing exactly how much time he had to get the ball to first base. Cal and Brooks made plays that were just phenomenal. Brooks won the 1970 World Series for the Orioles with his glove alone. It was mind-boggling how Brooksie would think and act so quickly in the field. The man has tremendous hands. I never could have done anything like that at third base. I had pretty good hands behind the plate with a catcher's mitt on. But this guy just had a glove on and stood in front of all those bullets and made it look effortless.

I see a lot of Brooksie in Manny. I would have thought Brooks would stay on the top of this list forever. But after watching Manny for a few years, I really do think that if he approaches the game as Brooksie did—intelligently and with dedication to his craft—he could be as good as or better than Brooks because of the fact he has a stronger arm. And offensively, Manny has the potential to be far better.

Now, keeping him on the Orioles team will not be easy. It depends on how much money Manny needs. That's what it's going to come down to. Agents in the game today are ruthless people. When they've got a guy who can put up the numbers that Manny does, they're going to squeeze the system as hard as they possibly can. Those kinds of situations are ruining the game of baseball. Manny, I just don't know. Is he going to want to stay an Oriole his entire career if we can't give him a $360 million contract? I'm not smart enough to know how that works.

**OUTFIELDERS**: Instead of breaking it down in left, center, and right, I'm picking the best three. **Paul Blair** made the most amazing catches that anyone could ever see. He played so shallow at Memorial Stadium and made up the difference when the ball seemed like it was going to go over his head. He could beat a team by himself with his defense. Paul had the stride, knew how to get a jump, knew what to look for. His knowledge of what to do before the hitter even stepped into the box was far superior to anyone I've ever seen.

I never thought that **Adam Jones** was going to fall into that category because he has a different ballpark to play in. It's tough to read the ball off the bat at Camden Yards because it travels better than it did at Memorial Stadium. Jones has learned to play the outfield as well as Blair, and we're not finished watching Jones make great catches in center field. He's got quite a few years left in him still. He's going to be in my top three of that list with Blair at the top.

**Frank Robinson** rounds it out. He was an MVP in both leagues. What he did offensively was incredible. All he did was bat .294 with 586 home runs and help the Orioles win the 1966 World Series. I never got a chance to really see him play, but how

Two of the best Orioles of all time, Brooks Robinson (left) and Frank Robinson (right), hang out with me prior to the 1983 World Series. (Baltimore Orioles)

can you possibly say that Frank Robinson wasn't one of the best outfielders in the history of Oriole baseball? He has to be.

**MANAGER: Earl Weaver** won 1,480 games with the Orioles. **Buck Showalter** is a distant second. Earl always said, "You practice perfect, you play perfect." And after a while, the mantra became how we lived the game of baseball. Earl would tell us about our weaknesses, and we had to adjust on our own. Every day we went out there not to beat the other team but to beat Earl because he pounded on us relentlessly on how perfect we had to be. There was no cutting corners with Earl. If you didn't do the job, he'd get someone else and he was not afraid to tell you that. There was no one else like Earl, and that is why the man is a deserving member of the Baseball Hall of Fame.

# Chapter 12

# From Behind the Microphone

My dream in terms of how I wanted my career to go would have been to finish up as a player, manage a few minor league teams, and become a manager in the big leagues.

After my playing days, I was a minor league manager for seven years. I got better at it, and down the road, that led to a job on TV with Comcast. Then I went back and coached with the Orioles from 2002 to 2006. It was a downtime for the organization. The team wasn't winning much, and what's worse, I hated working under Mike Hargrove.

Then Peter Angelos called me at the end of the 2006 season and asked me to do Orioles games on television for the Mid-Atlantic Sports Network, which he owns. So I had to make decision: should I come off the field and give up my dream to be a manager? That was hard for me to do because I figured I would be a major league manager, win a World Series, and then go into television. So the TV opportunity came a little sooner than I expected, but I had to be honest with myself. Peter always has had my best interest at heart, and when he advised me to take the television job, I decided, okay, I was going to give it a shot.

Like everything else I've done in my life, I was awful in the beginning. Broadcasting, though in particular, was as tough as anything I had ever done. After the first couple of years in this business, I almost quit. It was extremely frustrating, trying to understand the rhythm and timing of television, the pace at which you have to speak, the knowledge you need to make it all work. Every second counts when you're reading the spreadsheet for an upcoming show. It just did not work out real well. I was doing the pregame and postgame shows and I just didn't understand it. I couldn't get anybody to explain it to me. There were people in

It has taken a lot of hard work for me to become adept at broadcasting baseball games. (Baltimore Orioles)

MASN who were coming and going, which means there wasn't any consistency to it, and I really needed someone to tell me what this broadcasting thing was all about.

Finally, a pair of new producers came in, sat me down, and kind of beat it into my head what I had to do to be half-decent at this job. But I would be the first one to tell you: there were nights I went home with tears in my eyes because I just couldn't understand why I was so bad at it. I thank God for everybody in this company that was patient enough with me, hanging in there with me long enough until I finally got the hang of it. I don't think I'll ever be a great speaker and I don't have a good memory for names, which is part of this business. But I do understand baseball.

I understand the numbers, the complicated situations, reading hitters and pitchers and knowing what they're capable of doing.

I certainly know how to throw to certain batters. All that comes from the baseball field that I experienced as a player and a coach and a manager, and I know what goes through their minds to a certain degree. I never managed at the major league level, so I'll never really know how to deal with major league players in that regard. But just from listening to quite a few of my friends who are managers now, I have gotten a much better idea of how it all comes together. Knowing what I know now, I would be a much better coach and manager than I ever was. After watching some of the great managers of today, such as Buck Showalter, seeing them handle success and failure, I know what it takes to become a champion. Having played in dozens of postseason games, including three World Series, if I could just give the players of today the knowledge of what I've been through, there's no doubt in my mind that they would be championship players now. But managing a ballclub is no longer an option. I'm a broadcaster now.

I didn't want to disappoint Peter and fail as a broadcaster. I hired people to help me speak, to understand the television business. Although it took a lot of time, it finally became clear. I finally got over the hump after Tom Davis, who's now my partner in the booth, took me under his wing in 2009. He spent a lot of time with me, talking about some of the mistakes I was making and how to adjust my rhythm and timing. He talked about what questions to ask, when to talk, and when to keep your mouth shut. It finally started to work out for me.

I worked with two good people: Davis and Jim Hunter. But Tom really spent more time talking to me. His approach was a little different from Jim's. It helped me a lot when he broke it down to the smallest degree. At that point I started to feel a little bit of freedom to talk about things I knew. Everything started to come to me, and the things people wanted to hear about—my experiences, my knowledge, seeing the game through my eyes—came through on the telecast. But most importantly, you discuss the players every single day almost as if you're talking about your own children.

I understand it, too. I didn't come into baseball with a golden spoon in my mouth. I was a 145-pound catcher. But my work ethic enabled me to overcome a lot of obstacles. I asked a million questions to the point where people didn't even want to see me coming. But I asked the best players in the game about what it takes to become a great major league catcher. That's the approach you need in baseball, television, or anything. You need to seek advice and information from the people who are the best at this job. I don't think I'll ever be the best at doing interviews or that sort of thing, but when you ask me a question about baseball, it comes so much easier now than it ever did. I understand what's interesting to people, what it is that they don't see in a baseball game, and how to point that out.

It's different now than it ever was before because Tom relies on me for a lot of information. That's why I hate to miss a pitch during any game. Because if you throw a pitch in a certain situation, I know if it's the right or wrong thing you did, no matter what the outcome is, and how it impacts the game. Evaluating pitchers and hitters, all of that knowledge of the game, it's easier for me because I was lucky enough to play with so many outstanding teams. I know what a team has to do to win. The game comes to me very quickly.

I've been a coach in both the minors and majors and I know how hard it is for a coach to get through to certain players, especially in today's game. They have these big salaries, big egos, so you're walking on eggshells sometimes when you're around them. When you're a coach, you've got to satisfy the players, the manager, and upper management. Now, when I go into a clubhouse, I'm not there to judge anybody. I'm there to learn something about the players, and they are more than welcome to learn a little something from me—if they want. I would be more than happy to give them my take on it if anybody comes to me and asks, "What did you think of that play last night? What did you see?" But players are different today. They don't do that. I wore out Yogi Berra, I wore out Bob Rodgers, all of the coaches I had, about finding out how to be a really good major league catcher.

So now, I'm that person with the knowledge. I've been through a few stretches of successful baseball. I've handled quite a few successful pitchers, all those Cy Young Award winners, and I know what made them tick. I'd like to share some of that information if any one of those players would care to listen because I hate losing. When this team loses, even though I'm sitting in the booth, I feel like I'm losing, too. That's how much I love this team and this city. Just being around the Orioles for so long, it truly is my baseball family. I want to see them be great.

This job isn't simply about being in the booth and talking. I go into the clubhouse, I go down to the batting cage, to watch and learn. I'm not there all the time because I can sit upstairs and watch guys and see their approach to the game. I'd like to say some things to them. Of course, I wasn't a great hitter at the major league level, but I share with them what I saw great hitters do.

For instance, I saw how Eddie Murray approached batting practice and what he did in a game. In batting practice Eddie did not even think about hitting home runs. That wasn't part of what the game was all about to him. He went up there right-handed and left-handed with the ugliest batting stances you've ever seen like he didn't even give a shit whether the guy threw the ball or not. And then he just flipped at it, trying to cut a BP pitch down the left-field line left-handed. And when batting right-handed, he'd cut a fastball away to see if he could hit two or three feet inside the right-field line just over the first baseman's head. And he'd slap a ball up the middle once in a while or tomahawk a bad pitch. He would swing and miss sometimes, but he'd walk out of that batting cage with a smile on his face. Come game time, when the pitcher threw a nasty curveball to him, he'd flip it down the left-field line over the third baseman's head with the game on the line, and that's when it all paid off. He was the best clutch hitter I ever saw.

That's because his approach to batting practice was so damn simple: if the guy's throwing 60, 70 mph, why take a swing at the ball like it's game time and try to hit it 450 feet? It doesn't make sense. When they turn the dial up and say, "Play ball," Eddie turned the dial up, too. Ken Singleton was the same way. The last round, they might loosen a couple of swings, and maybe a few of those balls might find their way out of the ballpark. But you never saw them worrying about whether they had the power to hit the ball out of the ballpark in batting practice. They wanted to be able to adjust to the tough guys, the ones who came in and made nasty pitches to them, during the game. That's why they consistently beat the best pitchers in the game of baseball and made the Orioles a winning organization.

Speaking of Singleton, I talked to Singy, who is a commentator on the New York Yankees' YES Network, about the trade we're both in now. When I first heard Singy talk on radio and television, I wasn't very impressed with him. But after a couple of years, there was a transformation. He became very comfortable and very easy to listen to. I told him, "At first, you sucked, just like I did. What did you do?" Singy talked about how he spoke to people in the business. Announcing is an entirely different approach to a baseball game. *What's interesting to people? What should you focus on?* You listen to Jim Palmer speak, and the guy is such an eloquent speaker. I love listening to him talk baseball. Even when he discusses things that I didn't think were interesting, the way he puts it on television is captivating. That really helped me to be a little better.

My job with MASN is to break down a game and tell you what happened and why. I can mix stories in, but you don't get as much time to tell a full story. You can relate to something that happened back in my day—what hitters did, what catchers did, how they approached certain situations. But you can't spend a lot of time elaborating on it. You don't have that time in television.

Although I'm paid by the Orioles, I can be critical of the team if such criticism is expressed in the proper manner. I'm different than Jon Miller, who criticized a player to the point of being vicious. I think this is one of the things the organization protested about, asking him to be less critical of the players and to be a bit more positive about things. I was one of his pincushions. It got to the point where it was embarrassing for my family to listen to him during a game. He did the play-by-play for quite a few years and for him to make the jokes consistently got old in a hurry. I took offense to it. It caused quite a bit of animosity between Jon and me.

I learned from that. I don't think that's necessary. There are certain things that are worth bringing up—like something the organization is not doing right—but it's not my place to hammer that subject on a daily basis. Every year a team signs a lot of players, and sometimes mistakes are made. A player goes out on the field and doesn't look good, but you can't criticize the organization in every instance. The decision to sign the player was based on past statistics, performances, physicals, interviews. Sometimes it just doesn't work out. You don't overlook something like this completely, but by nature I try to look for the positives every day to keep the fans involved with this organization and with this team. You keep them on board, you give them hope. You don't give them despair. It's very hard to predict what's going to happen in this game, and often things can turn around in a heartbeat. There are too many variables, and if you start to predict what's going to happen, it will turn around on you in a second and make you look bad.

When it comes to analyzing a baseball team, I'm obviously going to be in tune with a catcher more than any player on the field. The catcher runs the game, relaying his knowledge and information to the pitcher standing out there on the mound. It took me a long time to learn how to call a ballgame and how to evaluate pitchers and hitters. I see things that aren't as good as they went for me, but I understand it takes time. If players don't make adjustments, it becomes frustrating. They think they're going to reinvent the game, but they aren't. And when I'm watching this, it bothers me. I want to say something to them, but that's not my place. I know Palmer can evaluate pitchers as good as anybody, and he'd like to share the knowledge with the pitchers on the Orioles. But they have coaching staffs that are trying their best to do that, even though some of them didn't have the opportunities—to be on the field for more than two decades—like Jim or I had. Still, it's very tough to offer your advice and prove your theories when coaches are trying their best to do exactly that. You have to be careful about your approach. You have to sit back, make yourself available, but don't force it on anybody. If they come to you, have an answer for them. But it's not my place to publicly criticize somebody for the way they do their job. I can give them a different perspective, but only if they ask.

I had a fire playing this game and I hated it when we lost. I took the things I learned from Weaver and the coaches and brought it into a game the best I could. When I see an inadequacy on the part of a major league player, when he doesn't see what he needs to see or make the adjustment that is needed, it angers me. I was always in this game to win. It was never, ever, about how much money I was going to make. I wanted to win from the first time I picked up a bat in Little League ball. This World Series ring I have on my finger, I wouldn't give it up for the money the players of today are making.

The game has changed in that respect. I don't see as many players today who are in it only to win. They want to win, but mostly it's about putting up numbers. Of course, the organization throws all the money out there that they need to put a good team together. But sometimes the players realize if they hit 30, 40, 50 home runs that they're looking at astronomical dollar signs. They're not going to sacrifice an at-bat to get a guy over to second or third base. You don't see those kind of players. They want the base hit and the RBI. But sometimes you have to sacrifice yourself with two strikes, hit the ball to the other side to get the runner to third base, and pass the baton to the next batter.

When a guy gets to the plate with a runner on second base and no outs, a right-handed hitter should be looking for a pitch in the middle or away that he can slap to the right side to get the runner over. I can tell when they take that first pitch that they're not thinking about it. They've just given away an opportunity to help the team. Very few players will go up there with that in mind. How many guys do you see go up to home plate without caring about striking out? They just go to their next at-bat. It used to be that you protect the plate with anything close when you have two strikes. We learn that when we're kids. That theory will never change. But it's about hitting the ball out of the ballpark now, driving in those big runs. Those are the things that will get you big contracts. There are players on the Orioles like that, and there are players on other teams like that. What ever happened to the hit-and-run? The squeeze bunt?

Then there's this: when the batter ahead of you in the order walks, you take the next pitch. You want to put as much pressure on the starting pitcher as you can. If he doesn't throw you strike one, you're just wearing him down. That's what you should be thinking about. It's not about guessing fastball and swinging at the first pitch and fouling it off. Pitchers are more vulnerable than they've ever been, and when the pitch count gets up there, he's out of the game. If you can make him throw more pitches, you're doing your job far better than swinging at that first-pitch fastball you know you're going to get. If you get a starter to 100 pitches, he's out of there. Then you're dealing with the bullpen. And you know why those pitchers are in the bullpen? Because they're not as good as the starter.

My job now involves more than just being on TV before the game and after the game. During the game I watch every pitch. I'm looking for patterns and I'm trying to find out how certain young pitchers handle certain situations. That gives me the knowledge of how to speak about them. If I see a pitcher adjust to a certain situation, then I can tell he's moving in the right direction. One of the most notorious situations this organization has is with the count at no balls and two strikes. I'm going to say 95 percent of the time or more, that hitter gets a hittable fastball. In our day the pitcher and the catcher both got fined if the hitters got a hit with an 0–2 count. But it taught you a lesson on how to approach that situation. You've got to be thinking, *I can get this hitter out without throwing a strike.* But if you don't care and they continue to get hits and home runs in those counts, that's one of the biggest mortal sins in baseball. This organization has just been horrible in that situation.

I feel what I do now is probably the best job in all of baseball. It's strictly your opinion, throwing it out there to fans who care about the Orioles. After all those years of being involved as a player down on the field—27 years, including the minor leagues and doing all the coaching that I did—to sit there and figure out what's going on is easy. There's not much preparation except for the statistics of the opposing team—who's hot, who's not, and all that bullshit.

The whole game has opened up to me by watching on television how the catcher calls the game. You can tell right away if the pitcher knows what his job is for the night or if he doesn't have a clue. You can tell what the catcher knows about the game—how to handle certain pitchers and how to pitch to certain batters. The whole thing is right there for me to see. And so it's easy for me to say what I need to because I was there for so freaking long. I've been in every type of pennant race you could imagine: on top of it all, a couple of games behind, scuffling to the finish line.

People want to know how a pitcher loses a game, throwing 97 mph with a nasty curveball. Sure, there are times when a pitcher doesn't get any support from his offense. Well, if that happens, you've got to throw a shutout. Kevin Gausman went 9–12 in 2016 but had a chance to win 15 games. He just didn't know how to do it. He didn't get any help on how to do it. There was a game in Texas on June 20 when we had a three-run lead against the Rangers, and he got into a 2–2 count with Bobby Wilson, the No. 9 hitter, and he refused to throw him a fucking curveball. And eventually the guy hit a sacrifice fly. Texas won 4–3. There's a point where he has

I really enjoy covering the Orioles for MASN with Jim Hunter, one of my many great colleagues. (Baltimore Orioles)

to take control of his own destiny in those games, and if he doesn't know what to do, it's nobody's fault but his own. Really though, has anyone ever said that to him? Palmer could tell you everything about every hitter on the other team. That's why he won three Cy Young Awards. Because he was smart.

Really, what I see is that the game hasn't changed that much at all. For instance, when thrown effectively, the fastball down and away is always going to be the best pitch. No catcher can ever forget that. What has changed is how teams set up their defenses. It's all very statistically based on where each batter hits the ball. We didn't have that in our day. We didn't go to the extreme they go to today. That stuff now is handled by computers and the brainiacs of the baseball world.

On the topic of the shift, I can remember a 2016 game when Adam Jones was at third base as the potential winning run with Chris Davis at the plate. The third baseman was playing near the second-base bag with two outs. A base hit wins the game, so you've got to bunt the fucking ball the opposite way. Slap the ball down, go stand on first base, and the game is over. It tells you about the mind-set of a player when he doesn't see that. Wow. That's the only thing that bothers me about the shift is that players don't have the ability to bunt the ball the other way. You've got to take the base hit because I guarantee you it hurts the opposing manager. I've seen Davis bunt a few times. Anybody can learn to bunt if you put enough time into it. You would think a guy of his caliber would work on that sort of thing. Now I'm not saying this specifically about Davis, but the players in today's game just want to put the numbers up. They're paying some pretty big dollars for home runs these days. But if he comes up in the bottom of the ninth, the Orioles are down by two runs, and they put the big shift on him, he's got to bunt the damn ball. You can't hit a two-run homer with nobody out there. A lot of players won't do that.

I worked 161 games in 2016. I missed the last one because I had to go home after my best friend died. Being on the field is good, but watching it on television can be better because the camera angles show you exactly where the catcher is moving, where he's giving his target, how he's calling the game, and what he wants from his pitcher. I sit back there and think about how great it would be if Matt Wieters had an earphone so I could communicate with him. I would tell him exactly where to move and what pitch to call. Knowing this pitching staff the way I do, we would have won this division easily.

One thing I learned from catching every day is that when you're thinking the game the way a catcher should think it and working a pitching staff, you are fucking exhausted when you walk into that clubhouse after the game. It has nothing to do with running down the first-base line to back up the throws. That isn't the type of fatigue that wears you out. It's trying to think ahead three batters all the time. *How are you going to get to that batter? What is he looking for in that second or third at-bat?* It's obvious to me from watching the games, watching on television, and having to report on this that they don't know these things. When I see the catcher move the wrong way, sometimes I start screaming, "Oh my God!"

Bud Norris was pitching for us in Philadelphia on June 18, 2015. We were leading 1–0, and there was a man on first, and Ryan Howard was coming up to hit. The catcher's got to know right away the situation and to tell Norris you can't make a mistake with this guy. You do it before the horse is out of the barn. We didn't do that. Perhaps they didn't want to waste time going to the mound. I say bullshit. I'm going to the mound 100 times if I have to. How can it ever be wasting time to go to the mound if it means winning the game? Just hustle out there and hustle back. So Howard came up, and Norris threw him a fastball—middle-in because we love the fastball middle-in. He swung and missed, and I thought, *If he makes contact, we're losing this ballgame.* You've got to think to yourself as a catcher, *That might not have been the smartest pitch, but I got away with it.* The next pitch was a fastball down and away, then it was a breaking ball underneath his hands, and Howard nearly fell over taking a swing. He looked like he'd never seen a breaking ball in his life. That sends a message to me. But the next five pitches were all fastballs, middle-in. He hit the fifth one out of the ballpark, and we lost the fucking game 2–1. We've given away 50 games like that, and it all comes down to not seeing what you need to see.

I feel we're not teaching our young pitchers how to take control of the game. That philosophy is gone from baseball. It used to be you show a pitcher the ropes, and then he throws the game he wants. There are certain principles you've got to teach them—how to control tempo, when and where to challenge a hitter. We should have done this ever since Jake Arrieta was here. Nobody really knew how to handle him, so we traded him away, and he became the best pitcher in baseball. We just didn't know how to help him get better.

Dylan Bundy showed great promise in 2016, but at this point, he really doesn't know what the heck he's doing. He's got incredibly good stuff, especially a great curveball, but does he know that because his change-up lacks movement that he really shouldn't throw it to the right-handers? He should go to his curveball; it's a better off-speed pitch.

Boston Red Sox star Mookie Betts hit three home runs off us on May 31, 2016, and then he came back here the next series looking for an encore. The first pitch was a curveball, and he took it. The second pitch was a curveball, and he swung at a ball a foot outside. So what do you think the next pitch was? Fastball. Betts hit a rope, fortunately, a two-hopper right at second baseman Jonathan Schoop. I'm thinking, *Are you crazy? If you're going to throw a fastball in that situation, use it to your benefit. Knock him off the plate, then come back with a breaking ball.* Giving him an opportunity to hit another home run with a fastball when he's already showed you he doesn't want to have anything to do with the breaking ball is a mortal sin to the game of baseball. Somebody should have said something to Wieters, and the pitcher also should have known better. You almost gave up a fucking base hit when you had him by the balls.

Our catchers need to get better. It's become an offensive position, but we fail to teach our catchers how to set up, how to receive a ball, and how to call a ballgame. We've lost all that. Gausman and Bundy, two of our best power pitchers, haven't really gotten that much better. It took all the way to the end of the season for Gausman to realize you need three really good pitches—and maybe even four—to win.

When's the light going to go on for these guys? That's the frustrating part about it because this is the fucking Baltimore Orioles. This isn't the San Diego Padres, some team that's always in last place and has no fucking clue what they're doing. We ought to be stepping ahead. We do everything well. We have the best relay team from the outfield that I've ever seen. We've been the best defensive team in baseball the last five, six years. And we've got the best closer, Zach Britton, to go along with Brad Brach and Darren O'Day. *And we have to scuffle to win this division?* There's something wrong.

That brings me back to my view from the booth. You don't see much from the dugout. You can't tell where the catcher is setting up. The best view is from right behind the pitcher, the view you get on TV. And if the pitcher and catcher aren't in tune, you're spinning your wheels.

We had a great season in 2016, but at the end, it looked like they were all swinging for the fences. They all felt like they were home-run hitters, thinking they were all going to hit 30 homers and drive in 100 runs. We just lost all that we put together. Jones was in and out all season long, waffling between being a good hitter and an undisciplined hitter. He has so much freaking talent that it's crazy. He's a Hall of Fame defensive player. He runs the outfield with an iron fist. You love to see that. At the plate he should never be afraid of being in a two-strike situation. But that's what it looked like because he knows he's vulnerable hitting with two strikes.

It becomes frustrating to me because I want to win, even though I don't play. I want to see Peter Angelos with a World Series ring on his finger. I want that for the players, too. I want to have that kind of pride in our team again because I love Baltimore. It's an incredible city, it's growing, it's getting better, and to have a World Series winner here would give this city back some of the character that it has lost. It's so much more fun to be part of a winning team and to be respected like it was in my day. It would be great to see that at Camden Yards. Man, the place is so beautiful, the best ballpark in the majors. There's nothing better than when the place is filled with fans cheering for the Orioles.

# ACKNOWLEDGMENTS

## Rick Dempsey

I would like thank all the people who took the time to help me along during my 24 years in the big leagues. From the beginning, Bob Rogers and Phil Roof with Minnesota, and Jim Hegan, a great catching coach with the Yankees, taught me many of the little things about catching that took me a long way in this game.

Thank you Thurman Munson, who inspired me by the way he played the game, and Cal Ripken Sr., who spent endless hours teaching me how to read hitters and pitchers, call games, give targets, think ahead, and take charge on the baseball diamond.

Thanks to all the great pitchers I caught from whom I learned so much: Jim Kaat, Dean Chance, Mel Stottlemyre, Catfish Hunter, Sparky Lyle, Mike Flanagan, Scott McGregor, Steve Stone, Dennis Martinez, Tippy Martinez, Orel Hershiser, and the best of them all, Jim Palmer.

Thank you to the managers I played for who made a definite impact on my desire to follow in their footsteps and manage someday in the big leagues: Billy Martin, a hard-nosed competitor but a players' manager all the way; Tommy Lasorda, an unrelenting winner who knew how to have fun at the same time (also, a great motivator and the best speaker I've ever heard, so good he could talk the devil out of hell); and then, of course, Earl Weaver. He was by far the toughest manager this game has ever known, but he proved every day that fundamentals are the key to winning, and you manage with your eyes, *not* your heart or a book. Although he screamed and yelled at me constantly and was by far the most miserable person to get along with, at the end of it all, I still loved him.

Thanks to the general managers and owners who gave me a chance and believed in me. That includes George Steinbrenner, who would do anything to win but respected all his players as long as they gave him 100 percent every day. Thank you to Orioles owners Jerry Hoffberger, who was so encouraging, and Edward Bennett Williams, a great and wise man. The same applies to general manager Hank Peters, who made the best deals of his time and stood up to Earl when he had to, and Dodgers general manager Fred Claire, a great believer in people and players and a man who had the courage to make bold deals. He won a championship in 1988 with the worst team on paper that reached the World Series. Thank you to Peter O'Malley, former owner of the Dodgers, and former Orioles general manager Harry Dalton.

Thank you Peter Angelos, a very good man and a smart businessman who brought me back to the Orioles and was always honest and up front with me. In our many conversations, he always gave me great advice and also provided me with the best position I could have at MASN. Peter is a very private person, and for that reason, people will never know how great he has been to me and the city of Baltimore.

Thanks to Chris Glass, executive producer at MASN, for your enduring patience and for sticking with me early on when I was absolutely awful on TV. Thanks also to Adam Martiyan and Michael Phillips for always having my back and supporting me on the set. Thank you Jim Hunter, my first partner, and a special thank you to Tom Davis, who helped me take it to another level in this very difficult profession. His mentoring, advice, professionalism, and friendship have been invaluable.

Thanks to my many friends in Baltimore who have been so supportive, helpful, and encouraging—most notably Todd and Diane Smith from Chestertown, who have always been there for me through some very difficult times. And thank you to Rick Oliver, who has been the absolute best agent/friend anyone could have.

Thank you Dave Ginsburg, the co-author of this book. It has been an absolute pleasure getting to know you. I appreciate your patience, professionalism, and your magic touch in bringing it all together. To the people at Triumph Books, who had the insight to put together Dave and me for the purpose of writing this fine book.

My thanks to the many Oriole fans who have put me on a pedestal I don't deserve. Playing baseball in Baltimore, along with living and working here, is my biggest joy.

And lastly, many, many thanks to my beautiful wife, Joani, without question the biggest reason behind everything good that has happened to me. She has always given me the freedom to pursue my dreams, no matter where they took me, and has given me a beautiful family of which I am so very proud. She has endured 47 years of me being on the road with tremendous loyalty. And yes, she still pretty much picks out all the suits and ties I wear on every show I do for MASN.

### Dave Ginsburg

The pleasure I derived from writing this book can be attributed in no small part to the patience of my wonderful wife, Cyndy, who allowed me the freedom to pursue this task by altering her schedule to fit mine. Thank you, Cyndy, for your unyielding support of my profession, especially during those brutal 10-game homestands.

Thank you to my parents, Jerry and Ethel Ginsburg, who teamed up to make me what I am today. Not only did my father take me to hundreds of games, but he also enhanced my love of sports by playing baseball, tennis, and football with me. Mom, a teacher, introduced me to the joy of reading by providing me with my first library card and buying, one by one, every book in the Hardy Boys series.

I wanted to be a sportswriter at an early age, and two prominent members of the Associated Press—the late Gordon Beard and the late Ira Rosenfeld—paved the way for me to be where I am today. I will forever be indebted to them.

Also, I want to mention baseballreference.com, which proved to be an invaluable resource to check and confirm statistics.

Finally, much thanks to Rick Dempsey. I can't think of a better person to collaborate with on my first book. What a pleasure it was, learning about baseball from one of the great Orioles and laughing uncontrollably at some of the wild stories he shared.